Guide to Establishing a Regional Health Information Organization

Edited by

Christina Beach Thielst, FACHE

LeRoy E. Jones

HIMSS Mission

To lead change in the healthcare information and management systems field through knowledge sharing, advocacy, collaboration, innovation, and community affiliations.

For more information about HIMSS, please visit www.himss.org.

About the Editors

Christina Beach Thielst, FACHE, is the Chief Operating Officer of Ventura County Medical Center and has over 25 years' experience in hospital and health administration. Since late 2003 she has applied her expertise with administration and governance as a consultant to several regional health information organizations (RHIOs), including the pioneering Santa Barbara County Care Data Exchange. She is also author of the popular Weblog, *Christina's Considerations* (http://thielst.typepad.com) and regularly posts on RHIOs and health information technology. In addition, she is the 2007 invited columnist for the *Journal of Healthcare Information Management.*

Ms. Thielst is a graduate of Louisiana State University and received a Masters in Health Administration from Tulane University, School of Public Health and Tropical Medicine. She is a Diplomate in the American College of Healthcare Executives. She is also an active member of Health Information and Management Systems Society, American Society Healthcare Risk Managers and serves on the Board of Healthcare Executives of Southern California.

LeRoy E. Jones is a Principal and Chief Executive of GSI, LLC in Philadelphia, an IT strategy, services, and consulting company. Through GSI, Mr. Jones provides products and services that are on the vanguard of the industry's collective agenda of moving information technology deeper into the care delivery process, with a particular emphasis on healthcare automation and data exchange. Mr. Jones serves as the Program Manager for the Health Information Technology Standards Panel (HITSP), an initiative to harmonize healthcare technical standards to enable interoperability among disparate health IT systems. Mr. Jones was also one of the inaugural members of the Office of the National Coordinator for Health Information Technology under the first appointed National Coordinator, Dr. David Brailer, extending a working relationship between Mr. Jones and Dr. Brailer dating back to 1996.

Mr. Jones holds an MS in Engineering in the Management of Technology jointly from The Wharton School and the Engineering School at the University of Pennsylvania. He received a BS in Computer Science from Carnegie Mellon University. Mr. Jones has served on the board of directors of Reboot Philadelphia and is a Certified Information System Security Professional (CISSP).

About the Contributors

Joseph E. Addiego, III, is a partner in the San Francisco office of the national healthcare law firm Davis Wright Tremaine, LLP. Mr. Addiego's HIT practice is focused on litigation, particularly with respect to disputes concerning software and hardware, and he is an active member of his firm's HIT and Privacy & Security practice groups. He also has handled numerous healthcare-related litigation matters. Mr. Addiego is the current Chair of the California State Bar Committee on Federal Courts.

Elaine A. Blechman, PhD, is Professor of Psychology, University of Colorado at Boulder. She founded Prosocial Applications, Inc., supplier of Caregiver Alliance Web Services™ and the Caregiver PHR (personal health record) system to long-term care consumers and RHIOs. She co-chairs the HITSP consumer empowerment workgroup, focusing on establishing interoperability standards that allow consumers to control and automate the exchange of data between their PHRs and their providers' electronic health records (EHRs). She has published eight books and numerous scientific papers about innovations in long-term care for individuals with chronic illnesses and disabilities and their families. With university and community partners, she evaluates the impact of PHRs on the coordination of long-term care (e.g., for cancer survivors, children with special health care needs).

Allen Briskin is counsel to the national health law firm of Davis Wright Tremaine, LLP, based in San Francisco, where he serves as a member of the firm's Health Information Technology Practice Group. Mr. Briskin's HIT practice is focused on community health information exchange network development and network user participation. He is a principal author of *Connecting for Health Common Framework: Resources for Implementing Private and Secure Health Information Exchange: Model Contract for Health.* Mr. Briskin has also assisted other firm clients in structuring information exchange pilot programs for comparative testing of new technologies, workflow redesign and evaluation of patient authentication, privacy, security and functionality components, conducting governance and organization surveys and, for Cal RHIO, developing a model agreement for regional network connectivity.

Howard A. Burde is a Partner and Health Law Practice Group Leader at Blank Rome, LLP. Mr. Burde represents health IT companies, health plans, and federal, state, and local governments. He routinely counsels in the areas of health IT, health insurance and managed care law issues, licensure, and certification and accreditation matters. Mr. Burde's wealth of experience includes seven years of service with the state government of Pennsylvania. Prior to joining Blank Rome, Mr. Burde served as Deputy General Counsel to Governors Tom Ridge and Mark Schweiker. From June 1995 until November 1997, Mr. Burde was Chief Counsel to the Pennsylvania Department of Health. Mr. Burde is the editor and contributing author of several books and articles, and serves on the boards of the *Journal of Health Law* and the *BNA Health Law Reporter*. As a graduate from the University of Virginia School of Law, he was a founder of the Virginia Health Law Forum.

Lorraine Fernandes, RHIA, is Senior Vice President, Healthcare Practice, Initiate Systems. She is responsible for leading the healthcare practice through defining healthcare trends and serving as a thought leader to the healthcare industry for patient identification and data exchange/linkage. Ms. Fernandes has more than 25 years of experience in the healthcare industry, 10 at large hospitals as director of medical record/HIM departments, including case management. A Registered Health Information Administrator (RHIA), Ms. Fernandes was the 1996–1997 president of the California Health Information Association (CHIA) and served on the organization's board of directors from 1993 to 1998. She received the CHIA Distinguished Member Award in 2001. Ms. Fernandes chaired the American Health Information Management Association (AHIMA) MPI Task Force in 1997, and was the recipient of the 1998 AHIMA Discovery Award. Ms. Fernandes served on various AHIMA committees from 1998 to 2005, and during 2003–2004 She served on the AHIMA FORE Board of Directors. Ms. Fernandes served on the 2004 Connecting for Health workgroup, Accurately Linking Health Information. Ms. Fernandes is also a member of HIMSS and is currently serving on the HIMSS RHIO Federation Workgroup. She speaks extensively on a regional, state and national level on issues of person identification and data exchange/linkage in the healthcare delivery system.

Steven J. Fox is a partner with Pepper Hamilton, LLP, a national law firm, serving clients throughout the U.S. He is resident in the firm's Washington, DC, office and leads Pepper's healthcare informatics initiative. Since 1990, Mr. Fox's practice has been primarily devoted to healthcare information technology. Beginning in 2000, for almost five years he wrote a monthly "Q&A" column dealing with HIPAA at HIPAAdvisory.com, and he is co-author of *Guide to Medical Privacy and HIPAA,* published by Thompson Publishing Group. He provides clients with legal advice and strategic counseling involving technology, e-commerce and healthcare information systems. In particular, he is experienced in the development, acquisition, negotiation, transfer and licensing of complex information systems, networks and software; outsourcing; EHRs, RHIOs, privacy protection, HIPAA; Internet and technology use policies; consulting/services agreements; and corporate, contractual and intellectual property matters. Mr. Fox is a frequent speaker and author on issues involving technology and healthcare information systems. He is also involved in many professional and industry organizations, including HIMSS (as an Advisory Board member), HIMSS' RHIO Work Group, American Health Lawyers Association, and Maryland HIMSS.

Todd Frech is Senior Partner at Ocius Medical Informatics, LLC, where he has completed projects for a wide variety of organizations including Pfizer Health Solutions and the California Department of Corrections. Mr. Frech specializes in health informatics with a focus on regulatory issues, system selection and implementation, and designing system integration strategies. Mr. Frech's career in health information systems spans 23 years and includes positions in healthcare organizations as well as in sales, marketing, account management, research and development, and operations in companies ranging in size from start-ups to Fortune 500 companies. Mr. Frech is a graduate of the Naval School of Health Sciences and completed postgraduate work at the Armed Forces Institute of Pathology.

Beth E. Friedmann, RN, MSN, is a clinical systems specialist at Long Beach Medical Center in New York. Her experience of over eight years in the management of enterprise system implementations spans both the business and health arenas. As a clinician, Ms.

Friedmann has specialized in pediatrics and neonatal intensive care and has served as a clinical nursing instructor at Adelphi University. Currently, Ms. Friedmann is a student in Columbia University's Biomedical Informatics program.

Gerry Hinkley is a partner in the San Francisco office of the national healthcare law firm Davis Wright Tremaine, LLP, where he co-chairs the Health Information Technology Practice Group. Mr. Hinkley's HIT practice is focused on community network development and finance, network user participation, system procurement, regulatory compliance and privacy. He has been involved with governance, network user and privacy projects for the California Healthcare Foundation, Connecting for Health (a program of the Markle Foundation and The Robert Wood Johnson Foundation), The California Endowment, CalRHIO and eHealth Initiative. Mr. Hinkley co-chairs the eHealth Initiative Working Group on Getting Started and Organization and Governance. Mr. Hinkley is an active member of The National Alliance for Health Information Technology, addressing regulatory compliance, governance and CPOE procurement initiatives. He also serves as a member of the Steering Group of Connecting for Health, the Certification Process Advisory Group of the Certification Commission for Health Information Technology, the eHi/HIMSS RHIO Federation Task Force, a technical advisor to the AHIMA State Level RHIO Consensus Best Practices Steering Committee, and has served as a faculty member at the Vanderbilt Center for Better Health, Privacy and Confidentiality Workshops.

Jeffrey P. Holmes has worked in HIT for the past 17 years across venues of care ranging from physician offices to hospital environments. As an active member of HIMSS, he has served on several committees including Advocacy, EHR and the RHIO Federation. He serves as liaison to a number of nationally recognized healthcare delivery systems exploring integration, HIE, EMR and rapid application development. Mr. Holmes is an employee of InterSystems Corporation, manufacturer of Cache´ and Ensemble.

Charles W. Jarvis, FACHE, is Assistant Vice President for Healthcare Industry Services and Legislative Affairs at NextGen Healthcare Information Systems. Mr. Jarvis' responsibilities include community and partnership business development including overseeing the company grants and funding procurement program, government relations, new business planning, and educational efforts. Mr. Jarvis is active in the Electronic Health Record Vendor Association (EHRVA), currently serving as Chairman of the Government Affairs and Affiliated Organizations Work Group. Prior to joining NextGen in 2005, Mr. Jarvis was in hospital and physician group practice management for 25 years in both the New Jersey and Massachusetts markets. Mr. Jarvis hold a Masters Degree in Business with a concentration in Health Administration from Temple University and a Bachelors Degree in Economics from the Wharton School of the University of Pennsylvania. He is also a Fellow in the American College of Health Care Executives and holds the American Medical Informatics Certification for Health Information Technology.

Laura Kolkman is the President of Mosaica Partners, LLC, a company specializing in providing consulting services to RHIOs and select healthcare providers. Prior to forming Mosaica Partners, Ms. Kolkman served as Vice President and Chief Information Officer for PharMerica Corporation. Before joining PharMerica, Ms. Kolkman was Sr. Director, Global IT R&D, at Pharmacia and Upjohn. Ms. Kolkman is actively involved with the Tampa Bay Regional Health Information Organization where she is a member of the RHIO Steering Team. Ms. Kolkman graduated Summa Cum Laude from the University of Michigan with a BSN in Nursing and earned an MS in Computer Science from Western Michigan University.

Keith MacDonald has over 20 years of experience in strategic planning, operations improvement, and research roles in ambulatory healthcare delivery. As a Research Director in First Consulting Group's Emerging Practices applied research group, Mr. MacDonald tracks and reports on operational best practices and the optimal use and benefits of information technology to support the ambulatory physician office practice. He has broad expertise in clinical operations and the clinical information systems that support an ambulatory physician practice through extensive consulting and market research experience in this arena. Prior to First Consulting Group, Keith spent 14 years at a large multi-site/multi-specialty physician practice, managing clinic operations, then as Director of Systems Planning coordinating information technology priorities and directing clinical system implementations.

David S. Szabo is a partner in the Business Department and Co-Chair of the Healthcare Group at the law firm of Nutter, McClennen & Fish, LLP, in Boston. He specializes in corporate and regulatory matters in the healthcare and life sciences industries. Mr. Szabo has made numerous presentations on HIPAA's privacy, security, and transaction requirements. He was a co-chair of the privacy & security subgroup of the New England HIPAA Work Group, Vice Chair of the Boston Bar Association's HIPAA Task Force, and a member of the steering committee of the Massachusetts Health Data Consortium Privacy Officers' Forum. He currently serves as chair of the Legal Working Group for the Massachusetts Health Information Security and Privacy Collaboration, and is a Director of the Massachusetts Health Data Consortium. Mr. Szabo is a graduate of the University of Rochester and Boston University School of Law, where he served as Executive Editor of the *American Journal of Law & Medicine.*

Peter T. van der Grinten, General Manager of dbMotion Inc., has over 30 years' experience in healthcare IT with a focus on medical record automation. As Vice President of Research and Development at HBO & Co. he oversaw the development of thousands of lines of code specifically dedicated to the development of the automated medical record; as COO of Simborg Systems, he was involved in the success of the HL7 protocol. He has extensive background in EMR usage and software development, HL7 experience and successful installations of hundreds of clinical systems for nursing, physicians, pharmacists and other clinical specialties. He has a BS in Computer Science with a minor in Healthcare Informatics from Purdue.

Jim Younkin is a Program Director of Information Technology at Geisinger Health System. He has 20 years of healthcare IT experience, including management of large implementation projects at numerous hospitals. Mr. Younkin is currently managing an AHRQ Implementation Grant project to develop healthcare information exchange between Geisinger and two community hospitals. He is also responsible for development of the Central Penn Health Information Collaborative (CPHIC), a newly established RHIO in central and northeastern Pennsylvania.

Contents

Foreword

John D. Halamka, MD
CIO, Harvard Medical School and CareGroup; CEO, MA-Share; and Chair, HITSP

There is ample evidence to suggest that a nationwide network of health data networks, linking together RHIOs from every U.S. town and region, would reduce healthcare costs and improve quality. Ideally, the lessons learned from existing successful RHIOs will provide a blueprint to building new RHIOs throughout the country.

However, as of 2006, there are only a handful of sustainable RHIOs performing live clinical data exchange. Each has a charismatic local leader, a locally defined business need, and a governance model that works well for the stakeholder participants in a local market. These RHIO models are each unique and have not been easily replicated in other regions.

This book, *Guide to Establishing a Regional Health Information Organization,* is the perfect cookbook for new groups seeking to develop a local RHIO customized to their marketplace.

In my experience, 80% of RHIO formation is governance, sustainability planning, and legal agreements for data exchange. Technology is only 20%. This book strikes a balance among these issues perfectly.

Christina Thielst begins with a discussion of building collaboration and developing local urgency to form a RHIO. I'm often asked to identify the reasons for RHIO success in Massachusetts. The trust we have developed through collaboration among payors, providers, patients and employers over 30 years is the most significant enabling force. Creating a driving coalition of interested stakeholders results in convening the RHIO discussion. Christina describes in detail how to initiate these foundational meetings.

Gerry Hinkley, Allen Briskin, Joe Addiego, and Steve Fox describe RHIO structural options and legal entity formation. In Massachusetts, we have a combination of 501(c)(3)s and limited liability corporations performing our RHIO activities. These legal structures have shaped the way we do business and were very important first decisions to prepare our RHIO for long-term survival and sustainability. Ensuring a new organization is governed through an open, transparent, inclusive process is the only way to develop trust in the community. The authors describe the risks and benefits of different governance models, so that each community can select a legal construct to meet their specific needs.

Beth Friedmann, Jeff Holmes, Todd Frech, Keith MacDonald, and Laura Kolkman discuss the critical topic of RHIO sustainability. No money, no mission. One of the greatest challenges of RHIOs is finding a set of products and services that the community is willing to fund at a level that covers the cost of providing services. Grants and government contracts are a short-term source of startup funding at best and create an ongoing operational liability at worst. Massachusetts used to have a rule that grant work must cover 40% of the cost of a project before we would consider applying. Now our rule is 100%. We will not take financial risk at the RHIO level and projects must have 100% sustainable funding before we will begin them.

Steve Fox, David Szabo, and Howard Burde outline HIPAA privacy and security implications for RHIOs. As a practicing emergency department clinician, I'm often told by outside doctors' offices and hospitals that data cannot be shared with me because of HIPAA. Many employees in healthcare do not understand HIPAA and the exemptions for payment, treatment and operations. It's clear that RHIOs must balance the protection of privacy, patient involvement in consent decision making, and the clinician need to know medical history to improve care quality. This chapter provides the background to inform local leaders who are addressing this balance.

Lorraine Fernandes and Jim Younkin discuss patient identification among organizations. In this country we do not have a national healthcare identifier and based on the Clinton administration's executive order precluding the discussion of this topic by the Department of Health and Human Services it is unlikely we will have a national healthcare identifier in the next decade. Thus, we must use other approaches such as a probabilistic combination of demographics. In Massachusetts we have implemented a record locator service for cross organizational patient identification using the methods Lorraine discusses.

Pete van der Grinten and Charlie Jarvis describe architectural and technology options for RHIOs. Healthcare information exchanges may be centralized or federated, patient identified or population based, used for primary patient care or secondary research users. The authors identify the various technology considerations that arose during a local RHIO implementation and provide insight into the issues to be addressed.

David Szabo and Elaine Blechman describe primary and secondary uses of clinical and financial data in a RHIO. Health information exchange in a community may take many forms: financial, patient-identified clinical data or de-identified population health data. Each type of data exchange has specific policy, privacy and technology challenges. The authors identify experiences from early RHIO pilots to highlight data exchange options and issues.

I hope you find this book as useful as I have. By leveraging the experience of all the authors, you can avoid repeating some of the expensive lessons learned in early RHIOs. I believe in a non-punitive approach to IT: open sharing of mistakes, failures, and painful implementations. In learning about the roadblocks encountered by others, readers of this book can create a path to their own RHIO that uses limited funds most efficiently and avoids the policy, privacy and technology mistakes others have made in the past.

Preface

Christina Beach Thielst, FACHE, and LeRoy E. Jones

While serving as the nation's first National Coordinator for Health Information Technology, David Brailer stated that rather than follow a business model with sustainable funding, the critical test for regional health information organizations (RHIOs) would be a governance model that brings in all stakeholders and includes established procedures for conflict resolution.

A recent HIMSS Vantage Point survey asked respondents to identify their biggest barrier to implementation of a RHIO; nearly half of the respondents identified the cost of development as a key barrier (Figure 1). In addition, 25% of respondents indicated that lack of organizational leadership was their biggest barrier. Respondents to the Vantage Point survey also noted that documents addressing infrastructure, data sharing and clinical data sets could provide substantial benefits for RHIO development. (See the HIMSS Web site, www.himss.org, for additional information.)

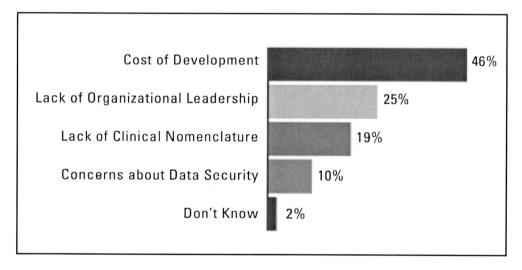

Figure 1. Barriers to RHIO Implementation*

This guide aims to provide practical guidance and information for building a viable RHIO that brings value to stakeholders and improves quality of healthcare for patients.

In a recent survey of 50 RHIOs conducted by the Health IT Transition Group, 48% reported being in the startup phase (Figure 2). These RHIOs are the ones most in need of resources such as this guide, which is a collaborative effort by a group of HIMSS members representing various disciplines who have been involved with RHIOs around

---

* From Vantage Point, April, 2006. Available at www.himss.org.

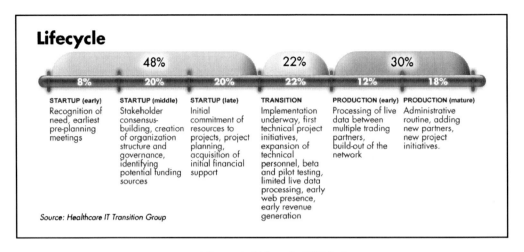

Figure 2. Lifecycle RHIOs*

the country. It attempts to provide a comprehensive set of materials to aid in the efficient and effective development and leadership of RHIOs.

While some might interpret the above characterizations of the current state of RHIOs as tenuous and the need for a guide like this one as confirmation of same, note that RHIOs have actually come a very long way in a short amount of time. When the term was first coined at the Office of the National Coordinator for Health Information Technology (ONC) in the bowels of the Department of Health & Human Services (HHS), it seemed so elegant and intuitive that it quickly became a tenant of the young health IT initiative: most healthcare is delivered locally, so most health data sharing would happen within geographic regions, and the local stakeholders in a given region should come together to make decisions about how that happened and how it was infused into local healthcare delivery. However, what seemed intuitive to some was anathema to others, and soon opponents rose up both within and outside of the government.

One hurdle for RHIOs was that there were seemingly competing terminology and concepts that were already established. ONC started talking about a Nationwide Health Information Network (NHIN) and RHIOs, and while not exactly the same thing, they sounded uncomfortably similar to the then-familiar concepts of National Health Information Infrastructure (NHII) and Local Health Information Infrastructure (LHII), which had considerable traction in the health information technology (HIT) circles. It quickly became apparent that these new ONC terms were being confused with the established concepts and continually required explanation on the distinctions. That led some to argue that there was no need for new terms, and that any distinctions there might be could be layered onto the existing concepts as refinements. Thus the term RHIO was almost assimilated into the HIT *lingua franca* of the day.

A second challenge RHIOs faced was one of jurisdiction. A number of organizations of various types were already involved in community data sharing initiatives that did not carry the RHIO moniker. The government was already funding various pilot efforts that had overlapping goals as ONC's new RHIO concept. Further, there were industry groups doing good work to make communities successful in their attempts to share

---

* From the Healthcare IT Transition Group. Used by permission.

clinical data, and a significant grassroots effort across the nation to try to get these kinds of efforts off of the ground. Some of these constituencies felt they neither needed nor wanted the Johnny-come-lately RHIO to brand, confuse or supplant their efforts.

A third challenge was a failed history of community health data sharing. Some HIT veterans recalled the early Community Health Information Networks (CHINs), infamous for their perceived failure to realize a mission similar to the RHIO cause. Eerily, the Clinton administration had put its weight behind CHINs in a manner reminiscent to the way the Bush administration was now backing ONC, and RHIOs by extension. Many wondered if RHIOs were destined to meet the same fate as CHINs, to be relegated to the fading memories of the HIT lifers as yet another disappointment in the effort to use technology to better healthcare. Analogies were made and many skeptics were vocal about the chances of success of a RHIO movement.

A fourth, and arguably the most difficult challenge was ONC's own questionable viability. Despite its name, ONC did not start out as an "Office" at all, but rather was the establishment of a position (the National Coordinator) with no staff. ONC had no natural home within HHS among the various operating or staff divisions. ONC had no budget of its own and was continually pressed down onto the budgetary chopping block. ONC had no physical real estate in the HHS building and had to live in borrowed quarters. ONC had very few seasoned government veterans, and had a team of largely government newbies at the helm who were often perceived as unorthodox and brash. The result was that anything this fledgling organization put forward was by definition suspect as a long-term proposition.

The saving grace for RHIOs turned out to be the national pulpit the ONC effort afforded for its evangelists to spread the RHIO gospel literally from coast to coast. In conference after conference, speech after speech, article after article, ONC's pro-RHIO agenda was preached again and again, and the industry began to take up the cause. Soon pre-existing community efforts started to self-designate as RHIOs; congressional staffers began to pen the term into nascent legislation; vendors started to market their wares as RHIO technology solutions; and some estimates of the number of RHIOs across the country were in the hundreds. The final test came when ONC staff suddenly appeared to stop mentioning the term RHIO, leading many opponents to quickly deem the term as dead. But like the eaglet that is pushed out of the nest to fly on its own, the RHIO concept had wind beneath its wings and has been flying high ever since as the industry pushed forward with the spread of RHIOs across the nation.

Therefore, the fact that we are even still talking about RHIOs as an industry, and that there are enough experts with real-world RHIO experience to assemble such a quality team as the one that produced this book, is a testament to the resiliency of RHIOs and a validation of the concept. This guide is like the energy bar a runner eats halfway through the marathon to give her strength to push toward the finish. RHIOs may not quite be in the home stretch in the maturity marathon, but they have come far enough that the distance ahead to the finish line is less than the distance back to the starting line. No matter where you are in your RHIO journey, we hope this guide will help you to finish well, and finish strong.

CHAPTER 1

Stakeholders, Collaboration and Driving RHIO Formation

Christina Beach Thielst, FACHE

This chapter presents the broad view of establishing a regional health information organization or network (RHIO, RHIN) and includes suggestions for getting started, establishing an opportunity statement to help clearly delineate the initial focus, identifying and building a foundation of stakeholders, and planning for a more formal leadership structure. This chapter also reveals some of the more common challenges facing those charged with the responsibility of forming a RHIO and offers a few recommendations for minimizing the magnitude of these challenges.

Getting Started

A RHIO can be described as a network of stakeholders within a defined region who are committed to improving the quality, safety, access and efficiency of healthcare through the use of health information technology (HIT). No two RHIOs look alike and each reflects the unique nature and interests of its region and resources. These organizations usually, but not always, form first as a collaboration of community visionaries bringing established organizations together to try something new. This creates the need to build trusting relationships and manage risk within a loose organizational structure.

Building and maintaining effective organizations and governing bodies takes commitment and work, especially in light of the Sarbanes-Oxley Act, Stark Laws and increasing Internal Revenue Service (IRS) and public scrutiny. Administrative and governance issues can sometimes pose the greatest risk and challenge to the ultimate success of these projects, so RHIOs must have leaders who can attend to these issues early in the formation process and continually monitor them as development of the organization progresses toward more formal models. The most effective leaders will drive RHIO formation by doing the following:

- Organizing, prioritizing and planning necessary steps;

- Setting target dates, assigning responsibility for each task, and holding individuals accountable for their commitments;
- Keeping a record of completed and planned tasks;
- Developing clear goals and strategies *(If you don't know where you are headed, you may never arrive!)*; and
- Making the case for why action is needed now.

The balance of this chapter reviews concrete steps RHIO organizers can take to begin the journey toward development of a connected community.

An Opportunity for Improvement

In the 1950s, W. Edwards Deming changed the lives of people around the world as a result of his visits to Japan in pursuit of quality. Since then his methods and techniques have been embraced in the U.S., and the interoperable exchange of health information is one opportunity for improvement that has been identified as a priority for the nation by President Bush. The President's establishment of the position of National Coordinator for Health Information Technology and Dr. David Brailer's appointment by HHS Secretary Tommy Thompson were the first steps in convening the National Health Information Infrastructure Initiative and establishing the project's leadership. The Framework for Strategic Action[1] served as the nation's opportunity statement. It is still being used to gain support from the many stakeholders and continues to be built upon by others joining the initiative. The numerous community networks exploring the feasibility of a RHIO in their communities represent quality improvement efforts and deserve recognition as frameworks for *local* action by stakeholders.

The following statement of opportunity will help those beginning the process of exploring or convening a RHIO by creating a simple descriptive statement that clearly lays out the scope and can help pitch the idea to stakeholders to get them engaged. As the shared vision and priorities emerge, the statement can be enhanced to form the community's framework for action.

> *An opportunity exists to improve the*
> *safety, quality, access and efficiency of healthcare*
> *by _____.*
> *We envision a scope that begins with*
> *_____ and*
> *ends with _____.*
> *The current system causes _____*
> *and improvement should result in _____*
> *for the _____.*
> *The process is important to work on now*
> *because _____.*

Once the statement of opportunity has been completed, RHIO conveners are ready to start recruiting collaborative partners from the community's pool of stakeholders.

Building a Foundation for Stakeholders

One of the first steps to take before identifying stakeholders is defining the community or region being served. Many connected communities have followed natural boundaries or historical referral/transfer patterns to establish the size and scope of their regions. Examples of existing regions, or organizing principles for healthcare communities, include:

- City
- County
- Multiple counties/parishes
- State/province
- Multi-state/cross-state
- Non-geographic population (disease, condition-based)

Once the geographic region or community has been established, conveners should begin to identify stakeholders, keeping in mind the following characteristics of a successful collaboration[2] and considering how those identified will impact the dynamics and contribute to the success of the RHIO:

- Shared goals and interests
- Inclusive governance
- Shared responsibility and input
- Shared ownership and commitment
- Trust
- Ongoing management and support
- Clear roles and responsibilities
- Ground rules for maintaining a safe atmosphere
- Active participation
- Balance of power and influence

Many RHIOs, because of their nature, will be collaborations of public and private health organizations that at times are competitors. The individual dynamics of the community, and the scope of the opportunity statement may dictate that all are welcome, or, in some cases with more limited scopes initially, the collaborative partners may be more selectively recruited. Either way, there are ten primary considerations for deciding who is sitting around your table.

1. Everyone should not look or think alike! Involve major players in planning, such as CEOs, COOs, CMOs, CIOs, nurse executives, legal counsel, and compliance officers, and avoid a narrow view. Stakeholders and collaborative partners should represent various disciplines, cultures, and perspectives, such as:
   - Clinicians and physicians
   - Community clinics and health centers
   - Consumers or consumer advocacy organizations
   - Correctional health clinics and hospitals
   - Employers
   - Federal health facilities (e.g., Department of Defense, Indian Health Service, Department of Veterans' Affairs)
   - Homecare and hospice providers
   - Hospitals

- Laboratories
- Long term care providers
- Medical groups and clinics (primary and specialty care)
- Medical, public health, and other colleges and schools
- Payors
- Pharmacies
- Professional associations and societies
- Public health agencies
- Quality improvement organizations
- State government (Medicaid)

2. Welcome "nay sayers" who can help you identify blind spots and minimize the possibility of "group think" tendencies. Seek out those who have expressed concerns and recognize that discussion, dialogue, and debate are part of the process. Identify concerns and their roots and explore solutions. You may learn something early on in the project which will save time, energy and resources. And you may even turn a foe (who can slow you down) into one of your most vocal champions. When this happens, you are usually rewarded exponentially!

3. The people sitting at the table during the formation period may very well evolve into the formal organization's governing body. As a result, take some time now to consider what will be needed in future board members and create profiles to ensure balanced representation and key strengths. A little planning up front in identifying the characteristics needed in future board members will help you build a strong board.

4. If you are just pulling together a collaborative project, start by assessing the community and preparing a description of its history. Consider using gathered information to geographically map assets of the community to help visually guide the planning process. Perform an analysis of the community's strengths, weaknesses, opportunities, threats (SWOT analysis) that addresses items such as:
    - Geographical issues
    - Stakeholder capacity
    - Community sources of pain
    - Stakeholder special interest(s)
    - Barriers/enablers/motivators to participation
    - Stakeholders

5. Build trust and prepare all stakeholders for *real collaboration*. During the exploratory process and early stages, identify and engage potential stakeholder representatives and assess their preparedness for cooperation and collaboration. Sometimes partners need to be reminded, and other times taught, how to work in a collaborative team environment.

6. Recognize that each organization participating in the collaboration will have its own culture and that others have little control over their actions. Invest some time communicating about organization-specific and cultural fit issues to minimize the risk of failure down the road.

7. Assess the leadership, facilitation, and communication abilities of stakeholder representatives and begin to recognize individuals assuming these key roles.

Effective leaders and champions of the project who can build trust, facilitate the creation of shared vision and goals, engage stakeholders, and communicate are vital to the success of a RHIO.

8. Plan for effective governance from the beginning by investing in building a team focused on the RHIO's mission and goals. There is work to be done and associated risk and cost(s).

9. The community has to *really* want the project, so after you describe what is envisioned for the project, ask stakeholders to sign a basic letter of support and commitment that communicates expectations and holds all accountable for their obligations. Once the organization is incorporated and has progressed in its development and formality, move toward use of Memorandums of Understanding (MOU) or business agreements.

10. The language and potential impact of health IT is new and sometimes misunderstood. There may be a valuable organization, or two, that needs more time and/or information than others before they feel comfortable joining the network. This may be especially true for consumers or their advocates. Consider assigning responsibility to one member who will continue to keep communication lines open and update the hesitant organization on milestones and accomplishments. Be prepared to provide the education necessary to advance their knowledge and understanding and extend a "welcome" to the table when they are ready to join with others.

Planning for Formal RHIO Leadership

As a collective group, the governing body is responsible for accountability, authority and oversight. Many RHIOs start with a project steering committee whose members represent the founding collaborative partners. However, the need to establish a formal organizational and governance structure will arise as the number of partners increases and the collaboration begins to bring clinical and technology plans into focus and looks toward implementation and oversight. Two popular markers for when it is time to incorporate and establish a legal governing body include the desire to hire staff and apply for and receive grant funds. However, an effective collaboration will have assessed governance needs much earlier in the process to make the transition to a formal structure smoother, including:

- Recognizing the position of the RHIO, its distinct place in the healthcare market of the region, and areas of overlap or competition with other organizations;
- Identifying formal and informal community leaders and project champions and foes;
- Identifying and engaging stakeholders with passion and developing new champions of the project *(Tip: Bring potential champions into the process in any capacity, whether on the governing body or as members of committees or advisory groups.)*;
- Identifying stakeholder representatives who can serve on a board and be accountable to the community as a whole, and not to their individual interests;
- Ensuring a shared vision and mission among those involved with the project;
- Finding a place in the organization for clinical, technical, and administrative (financial, management, legal, etc.) contributions;

- Identifying a pool of advisors that can help the collaborative partners through challenging times; and
- Considering options in organizational and governance structures with systems to ensure accountability and sustainability for the benefit of *all* stakeholders.

When recruiting members to sit on the formal organization's board, define responsibilities and do not minimize the role or its requirement. Provide for candidates a written board member description and other information about the organization and let them know what skills, abilities, and strengths they are expected to bring to the project.

If the new board plans to hire staff, members will need to explore their attitudes toward the delegation of the management of the organization and build trusting relationships with the executive director and other staff. The new board will ultimately delegate the management of the organization, but not responsibility for oversight. According to John Griffith "the executive office supports the governance system both in facilitating the decisions of the governing board and in seeing that the board decisions and plans are effectively implemented."[3]

The new board will want to consider securing an IT professional or identifying a chief information officer who can effectively represent the interests of the community and project and contribute to planning. Board members will realize the true value of this role as they begin to engage technology vendors to evaluate products and options and transfer their vision into operational plans.

The new board members will also want to establish measurable and achievable goals and evaluate options in financing and funding models to sustain the new organization. Relying on data to drive their decisions will contribute to more effective planning and increase the likelihood of successful funding applications and the ability to demonstrate value, quality, safety, and cost benefits to contributors.

Getting Down to the Business of a RHIO

When establishing a new RHIO, there is much to discuss and some boards or committees may find themselves bogged down in details or straying off of important topics. To minimize this risk, collaborative partners should insist on effective meetings that start with a prepared agenda, time allotted to each item, and a designated person(s) responsible for facilitating that discussion. The first order of business for any new group should be establishment and/or review of ground rules for member behavior. Next, prioritize agenda items and allocate time to each one as appropriate. When the time for each agenda item expires, move on to the next item. If a new issue arises or an item needs additional research or discussion, consider use of an ad hoc team to explore the issue in more detail and report back at the next meeting.

Starting a new project, a new strategy, or even moving from one step to the next can sometimes be overwhelming. One tool to help the new governing body experiencing difficulty moving from one step to the next is talking with advisors and another is applying quality improvement tools such as the Shewart Cycle (Plan-Do-Check-Act), as shown in Figure 1-1.[4]

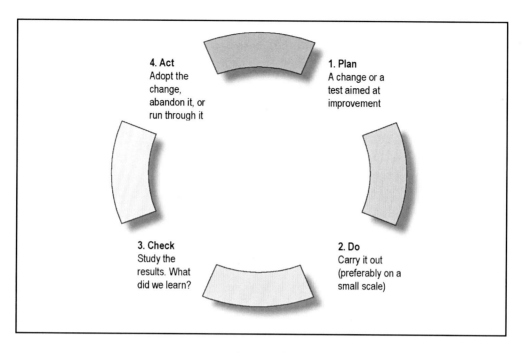

Figure 1-1. The Shewart Cycle (PDCA)*

Dr. W. Edwards Deming, known as the founder of the new economic and industrial era, often noted that when the Plan-Do-Check-Act (PDCA) cycle was being used years ago by Walter Shewart, it was known as the "Plan-Do-Study-Act" cycle (or even the "Shewart Cycle"). Although PDSA may be more applicable, PDCA is firmly rooted in quality improvement language.

Plan: Refer to your improvement plan; have team members discuss their readiness to begin the next stage or step. What have you learned so far? What should you do next? What understanding or skills will your team need in the next stage? How will you learn what you need to know? If the team is reluctant to move to the next step, identify potential reasons for the floundering. If you have no improvement plan, create one, starting with an opportunity statement.

Do: Make some early attempts at the next steps in the strategy or plan you are following. Allow yourselves to make mistakes.

Check: Reflect on your trial efforts and identify ways to improve them. What worked or went well? What did not work well? What resources, training, or knowledge do you need to do a better job? Can advisors help you fulfill these needs?

Act: Have the team discuss how to incorporate the lessons learned from your trial runs. Repeat the early steps including these improvements.

---

* Adapted from Scholtes PR. *The Team Handbook: How to Use Teams to Improve Quality.* 1991.

Challenges Facing RHIO Formation Leaders

Conveners and leaders of RHIO efforts must be prepared to address challenges that arise as a result of any collaborative process and the exchange of private health information. Some common challenges to anticipate are as follows:

General
- Fear of loss of advantage
- Individual stakeholder priorities
- Lack of trust and accountability
- Maintenance of interest and buy-in
- Motivation
- Politics—finding "neutral" ground
- Pride of ownership

Business / policy issues
- Competition between stakeholders
- Consensus of common policies and procedures
- Consumer privacy concerns
- Costs—financial and personnel—especially for small/rural providers
- Decreasing debt capacity
- Difficulty in reaching multi-enterprise agreements for exchanging information
- Financing
- Governance and leadership
- Other economic factors
- Physician and payor incentives
- Return on investment
- Sustainability
- Transparency of process
- Uncertainties regarding liability

Technical/security issues
- Accommodation, conversion, or discarding of legacy systems
- Auditability
- Authentication
- Interoperability among multiple parties
- Security and legal issues
- Standards
- Vendor lock-in vs. vendor agnosticism

Internal to the collaborative partner's organization/RHIO
- Competition for resources
- Dilution of effort: project competing against other pressing needs
- Increased cost of IT (perceived or real)
- Preservation of previous investments

External to the collaborative partner's organization/RHIO
- Business continuity: destruction/recoverability of critical resources
- Lack of accountability and control (perceived or real)
- Linking outside: standards, reliability, controls
- Reliability of data: potential mismatching of patients and data corruption
- Rights in data: who "owns" the data and who can make changes (tracking changes)
- Security: data and physical resources

Suggestions for Overcoming Challenges

It is important that collaborative partners and leaders of the RHIO effort find ways to overcome these challenges, and possibly view them as opportunities for improvement. Some suggestions include:
- Keep the patient and security and privacy of their information at the forefront.
- Do not become overwhelmed by the long list of challenges.
- Obtain buy-in from the highest level of each partnering organization.
- Engage state and national leadership and continue the dialogue, provide education on local issues, and gain their support.
- Identify effective leaders and champions.
- Identify financial incentives to promote provider investments in their internal systems.
- Identify funding options for information technology and RHINs/RHIOs.
- Explore the needs of rural and small providers and possible solutions.
- Leverage the efforts of the larger health systems and promote collaboration, not competition.
- Educate and communicate with partners, advisors and the community.
- Recognize opportunities and plan some quick "wins."
- Build on improvements in the ease of inter-institution partnering.
- Identify the value and benefits that accrue to each partner and stakeholders.
- Adopt common terminology and establish standards.
- Spell out all interface and data specifications in excruciating detail, and hold everyone to them.
- Address adjudication of liability and continually monitor the agreement structure (letters of support, memorandums of understanding, agreements, contract).

In summary, the most effective RHIOs will be those with champions and effective leaders whose collaborative partners maintain a shared vision, remain organized, plan well, and stay focused. They will be inclusive of all stakeholders and share their stories of success with the community they serve. But most importantly, the collaborative partners will remain focused on the needs of patients and not their own individual interests.

The next chapter will detail the options and necessary considerations related to formal RHIO governance structures.

References

1. Framework for Strategic Action. Available at www.hhs.gov/healthit/strategicfrmwk.html.
2. UCLA Center for Health Policy Research. Health DATA Program Workbook. 2004. Available at www.healthpolicy.ucla.edu/HealthData.
3. Griffith J. *The Well Managed Healthcare Organization, Fifth Edition.* Chicago: Health Administration Press; 2002.
4. Scholtes PR. *The Team Handbook. How to Use Teams to Improve Quality.* 1991.

CHAPTER 2

Entity and Governance Models for RHIOs*

Gerry Hinkley, Allen Briskin, Joseph E. Addiego, III, and Steven J. Fox

This chapter provides a practical "how to" approach for RHIOs to address the process of establishing a formal RHIO governance structure and through that structure evaluating whether a new separate entity is appropriate to house RHIO assets and operations and to conduct RHIO business. The authors stress the importance of sound business planning for the RHIO, which is an essential first step to entity and governance planning and drives much of the decision-making in this regard. As in the previous chapter, this chapter also stresses the importance of engaging qualified leadership, involving necessary stakeholders, and establishing a detailed work plan and realistic time frame for the process.

Where a new, separate entity is called for, this chapter provides a basic understanding of the different entity forms, both corporate and non-corporate, that should be assessed in connection with selecting the type of entity. If a new, separate entity is not appropriate, the chapter also describes how a RHIO could be organized through multiple contracts as a virtual entity.

Once the type of entity is selected, the chapter then turns to development of an appropriate governance structure. The governance structure is set forth in bylaws of a corporation, in the operating agreement of a limited liability company, the partnership agreement of a partnership, the enabling legislation of a public body, or the contracts among stakeholders in a virtual entity.

Tax status for RHIO entities is a complex subject, and, like governance and entity selection, requires analysis specific to the RHIO's unique circumstances. This chapter provides general introductory guidance with respect to the attributes of taxable, tax-exempt and nontaxable entities and describes the bases for tax-exempt status and non-private foundation status.

---

* The information contained in this chapter is illustrative only and is not intended, nor should it be used, as a substitute for specific professional advice that can be given only in response to inquiries regarding particular situations. You should not act upon this information without seeking professional counsel.

In a final section, the chapter demonstrates how an effective governance process can address the issue of system procurement.

The Entity and Governance Structure Planning Process

Entity and governance planning should begin at the very outset of RHIO organization and should be conducted in tandem with the formalization of the organization's business plan. A preliminary governance structure will evolve as leadership and key stakeholders willing to supply volunteers are identified and begin to engage in the initial planning activities. The initial leadership team will be relatively self-evident; however, they should identify and recruit other individuals with additional skill sets needed to achieve the RHIO's immediate goals.

Stakeholders

The RHIO's power, credibility and authority will be derived primarily from the group of stakeholders. Initially, expect a core group of conveners to emerge. Conveners will recognize at the outset of planning that they have a vested interest in the RHIO and believe that joint activity through a RHIO will achieve interoperable health information exchange in the RHIO's market and enable the RHIO to become a component of larger networks. Conveners should identify and engage the larger stakeholder group through their own contacts, word of mouth, and more formal means, such as surveys and focus groups. The conveners should provide meaningful opportunities for representatives of professional and institutional health care providers, employers, third party payors, governments, funding sources, technology vendors and consumers to participate. Some necessary stakeholders may not be willing participants; however, to ensure the RHIO's credibility, obvious stakeholders should not be left behind. This is not to say that every stakeholder needs to be in the room when every major decision is made. In addition to governing body membership, stakeholder participation can be accomplished through active involvement in working groups and also through regular reporting to stakeholders by RHIO leadership and formal solicitation of stakeholders' input through advisory bodies.

Survey Tools

The conveners should survey stakeholders to identify issues and clarify positions that may influence governance structure decisions and the development of a work plan for developing the RHIO. The data gathering process should address the following subjects:

- The mission of, and objectives and/or gains to be achieved by, the RHIO;
- Key issues for developing the RHIO, in both initial organizational and subsequent operational phases;
- The organizations and individuals that should be involved in organizing, governing, and advising the RHIO; and
- How the RHIO will finance its organization and operations.

Data gathering may be a multi-step process, through which a relatively large number of individual stakeholders are surveyed regarding core issues, and selected participants are invited to respond in greater depth. An example of a two-part survey tool is presented in Appendix A: Governance Issues Survey Tool.

Work Plan

The form of the preliminary governance structure should be driven by specific short-term goals that are clearly enunciated in a work plan with at least the following tasks:

- Identifying and enabling stakeholders;
- Establishing formal working groups to address governance, business planning, and sustainability and technology;
- Defining the activities that the RHIO will engage in initially and ultimately;
- Identifying potential sources of funding and ways for the RHIO to achieve sustainability;
- Evaluating options for an appropriate form of entity, desired tax status and governance structure;
- Defining entity and governance objectives and principles for the RHIO including the following:
  - Characteristics of the form of entity (or non-entity) chosen for the RHIO, such as its ability to be tax-exempt, perpetual, have a membership, and its relationship to constituents and government entities;
  - Governance tiers, including founders or third parties with certain reserve powers, members, governing body, officers, executive management, advisory groups, funders, RHIO customers, and consumers (see Appendix B: RHIO Entity and Governance Objectives and Principles); and
- Establishing the organization and a stable long-term governance structure.

Leadership Team

Inasmuch as the RHIO is essentially a start up technology-based initiative, a well-rounded leadership team should be equipped to address and comprehend the relevant market for the RHIO's services, necessary functionality, potential technology solutions, the technology procurement process, business models, seed funding and revenue sources, staffing and consulting needs, the political environment for RHIO development, and the potential for strategic partnering. Just as important, the leadership team should include individuals who are capable of overseeing execution of a thoughtful communications plan and who have recognized clout in the region. Gaps in the skill set of the leadership team can be filled by volunteers or advisors not able to devote substantial time and effort as leaders, but available to assist on specific issues, or by consultants experienced in business planning, technology procurement or legal and regulatory issues.

Volunteers

Many RHIOs rely on volunteers to sit on governing bodies, working groups, and task forces. Initially, it is desirable for senior executives to be involved to empower the process. However, care needs to be taken to utilize the time and effort of these particular volunteers or the RHIO will risk losing them along the way. To accomplish this, RHIO staff and delegates of senior executive volunteers should be engaged to do the necessary groundwork to properly prepare the background for ultimate decision-making. Issue papers reflecting the efforts of staff and delegates demonstrating sound bases and thorough analyses underlying recommended alternate courses of action should be prepared and distributed well in advance of key meetings. In addition, discussion leaders should be identified and fully briefed beforehand to ensure that key volunteers are appropriately engaged in making decisions. All of this should be carried out pursuant to a timetable that is published at the outset and adhered to strictly.

Documentation

Regardless of the composition of the leadership team, as supplemented by others, the leadership should be careful to comprehensively document the start up decision-making process and results to ensure that there can be effective knowledge transfers to individuals who will provide ultimate RHIO leadership. It is unlikely that the ultimate leadership team will all have been present during the RHIO's start-up phase.

Organizational Models for RHIOs

Several models for RHIO organization have been suggested. These include nonprofit or mutual benefit corporation, for-profit general law corporation, limited liability company or partnership, special district or authority, and joint powers agency. A description of each of these forms follows. In addition to determining which form of entity is appropriate, the planning process should address whether an existing entity might be more suitable for the RHIO than a new entity. If a new entity is to be utilized, the planning process should consider whether use of an incubator or fiscal agent would be an appropriate transitional model. How incubators work is discussed in this section, which also covers the potential utility of a "virtual entity" in place of an existing or new entity. The end of the section describes a tool for evaluating the models that have been identified as potentially applicable to the RHIO.

Nonprofit Public Benefit Corporation

A nonprofit public benefit corporation may be formed for any public or charitable purpose, provided its assets are irrevocably dedicated to that purpose. Articles or a certificate of incorporation is filed with the Secretary of State of the state of organization to commence the corporation's existence. Governance of the corporation is as set forth in bylaws adopted by the founders. The corporation may have members, but is generally not required to have members. Its business is conducted under the ultimate authority of a board of directors. The directors can be elected by the members, although, as provided in the governing documents, directors may be designated by nonmembers. Directors may also serve by virtue of their holding a designated position with another organization. Such directors are said to serve *ex officio*. If the corporation has no members, the board of directors is often self-perpetuating. The officers of the corporation are charged with responsibility for day-to-day management and report to the board of directors.

Inasmuch as the assets of the corporation are dedicated to charitable purposes, the assets are considered to belong to the public and the state attorney general is authorized to act on behalf of the public to protect the public's interest. The status of a nonprofit public benefit corporation to have its income exempt from tax can be established through application to the Internal Revenue Service (IRS) and the corporate taxing authority of the states in which it conducts business. Mere formation of the corporation does not achieve tax-exempt status. Rather, the corporation must apply for and obtain recognition of exemption from both the IRS and their state. Organizations that are organized and operated exclusively for charitable or public purposes may seek exemption under section 501(c)(3) or 501(c)(4) of the Internal Revenue Code (IRC; the Code). (See below.)

Nonprofit Mutual Benefit Corporation

A nonprofit mutual benefit corporation is an appropriate organizational form for cooperative ventures among entities in the same industry. This type of corporation may be formed for any lawful purpose, provided that purpose is for the benefit of its members. Governance of nonprofit mutual benefit corporations is similar to that of nonprofit public benefit corporations, except the corporations are required to have members. The assets of a mutual benefit corporation are not irrevocably dedicated to public and/or charitable purposes. Thus, unlike a public benefit corporation, a mutual benefit corporation can typically, upon dissolution (or in connection with the repurchase or redemption of memberships), distribute corporate assets to its members. A nonprofit mutual benefit corporation is not eligible for recognition of exemption from taxation under section 501(c)(3) or (c)(4) of the Code. However, it may seek recognition of exemption under section 501(c)(6) of the Code. To qualify for an exemption from taxation, the corporation must be established to promote a particular line of business and no part of the corporation's net earnings may inure to the benefit of any private individual. A line of business may be narrowly defined but must be fully representative of the entire line. Thus, an association of healthcare providers in a particular region would likely qualify for exemption, whereas an association of providers associated with a single hospital organization may not.

For-Profit General Law Corporation

A for-profit general law corporation is a useful organizational form when those who provide the capital for the organization require measures to ensure a return on their investment. A for-profit corporation generally may be formed for any lawful purpose, other than a small number of specialized purposes governed by specific regulatory frameworks (e.g., banking, performing medical or other professional services in states that prohibit the corporate practice of medicine, etc.). Like nonprofit corporations, for-profit corporations are created by filing articles or a certificate of incorporation with the appropriate state's Secretary of State. Bylaws provide for the organization's governance. For-profit corporations issues shares of stock to those who contribute money, property or services to the corporation, and these shareholders elect the corporation's directors.

A for-profit corporation's shareholders may receive a return on their investment through distributions of dividends, or through sales of their shares of stock to other parties.

For most legal purposes, a corporation typically is treated as a separate entity from its shareholders. As a result, a corporation's shareholders are not responsible for the corporation's, or each other's, obligations and liabilities.

Partnership or Limited Liability Company

A general partnership is an association of two or more persons to carry out a business on a for-profit basis as co-owners. A partnership is formed when the partners agree to do business as partners and is governed by the terms of that agreement. Typically, partners form a partnership by entering into a written partnership agreement. As a general rule, a general partnership is governed by its partners and not by a separate board of directors, although the partnership agreement may provide for certain aspects of the management of the partnership's business to be delegated to a management or similar committee or to a managing partner. A partnership and its partners are not treated as separate legal entities for certain purposes. Most notably, the partners of a general partnership are ultimately responsible for the obligations and liabilities of the partnership.

A limited partnership has two classes of partners. General partners participate in the management of the partnership's business and are ultimately responsible for the partnership's obligations and liabilities. Limited partners do not participate in management, but also are not ultimately responsible for the partnership's obligations and liabilities. The formation of a limited partnership is generally somewhat more formal than for a general partnership, as state laws typically require the filing of a certificate of limited partnership with the Secretary of State. A limited partnership's governance is controlled by the partnership agreement among the general and limited partners.

The limited liability company (LLC; also known as a "limited liability partnership" in some jurisdictions) is a relatively modern form of organization that is similar to a limited partnership in a number of respects. A limited liability company is formed by the filing of articles of organization with the appropriate Secretary of State. A limited liability company's owners are referred to as "members." The limited liability company's business may be managed by its members or by one or more other parties referred to as "managers," depending upon the terms of an operating agreement among the members. In a limited liability company, the operating agreement generally serves the same purpose of the partnership agreement in a general or limited partnership. Unlike a general or limited partnership, however, a limited liability company has no general partners. Thus, neither the company's members nor its managers, if it has them, are ultimately responsible for the company's obligations and liabilities. In this respect, the members and managers of a limited liability company are shielded from liability to the company's creditors in the same way that shareholders and directors are shielded from liability to a corporation's creditors.

Special District or Authority

State laws may permit the formation of regional or state-wide governmental or quasi-governmental agencies authorized to act for specified purposes or to conduct specified activities. For example, California's Healthcare District Law provides for the organization and operation of local government agencies that may operate hospitals or carry out a broad variety of other activities to promote healthcare in the communities they serve. The rules governing the organization and operation of a special district or authority will vary significantly from state to state. These rules will be specified in the state's constitution and/or in its statutes. These laws generally describe the process by which a special district or authority may be formed, such as by the holding of an election in the communities it would serve or by action by the state legislature. A special district or authority typically is governed by a board of directors or similar body, the members of which are either elected by the voters and/or appointed by other government officers, such as the governor or local county board of supervisors.

The special district or authority's powers will be dictated by the state's laws and/or by the charter or statute that is adopted to form the district or authority. A special district or authority may have funding resources that are not available to a private entity such as a corporation, partnership or limited liability company. For example, a special district or authority may have the power to raise funds by issuing bonds. Moreover, a special district or authority may have the power to assess taxes upon those who live or own property within its geographic boundaries, or to receive a share of tax revenue collected by other branches of state or local government, such as sales and use taxes or the state's general fund.

Joint Powers Agency

State laws typically allow for a cooperative arrangement by and among existing public agencies. This model brings together multiple agencies under a new and separate public entity but does not allow for participation by any non-governmental participants. Upon approval by the legislature or other designated body, the parties enter into a joint powers agreement to govern the terms of their cooperative arrangement. Typically, each member of a joint powers agency must be able to independently exercise the power which is exercised by the joint powers agency. Although the agreement may establish specific conditions and terms that limit each agency's ability to act independently, it does not alter the basic structure of each agency's decision-making processes. The new authority has a separate operating board of directors. Every new authority must meet certain organizational requirements of initiating a new governmental jurisdiction. A joint powers agency may qualify for exemption from taxation under Internal Revenue Code section 115, which excludes from taxation income that accrues to states and political subdivisions that is derived from the "exercise of any essential governmental function." Whether a particular activity is deemed an "essential governmental function" is determined on a case by case basis, but income that is an integral part of the state or its political subdivisions is generally not taxable unless there is a specific statutory authorization for taxing its income. In some states, special legislation may be pursued to allow for the formation of a joint powers agency that includes non-governmental participants. The tax exemption rules that apply to a joint powers agency, also apply to a special joint powers agency.

Existing vs. New Entity

In connection with determining the appropriate form of entity, the planning process should consider the potential use of an existing entity. It may be that an existing entity would be in a position to more aggressively implement the RHIO business plan because the necessary organizational infrastructure and sources of capital would already be in place. However, an existing entity may also have "baggage," such as perceived favoritism toward one or another constituency that could belie the organization's potential to be accepted by a broad constituency. Some additional potential advantages and disadvantages of using an existing or new entity are identified in Table 2-1.

Each advantage and disadvantage is not weighed equally; some are more critical than others. In determining whether an existing or new entity should be used, the project team should place more emphasis on the model that allows for:

- Greater neutrality;
- Timeliness in becoming operational; and
- Economies of scale.

Possible candidates as existing entities to carry out a RHIO's purposes and activities include:

- **Trade Associations.** Trade associations, such as hospital associations and medical societies, will have a pre-existing interest in RHIO purposes. However, placing RHIO functions in one of these entities could result in the RHIO entity focusing too heavily on the issues of the particular trade association to the detriment of the other issues.

- **Regional Technology Consortia.** Geographic technology consortia have been formed in concert with local and state governmental initiatives. Such consortia may have purposes and activities closely aligned with RHIO purposes. However, as with trade associations, regional consortia may suffer from being single-subject focused and lacks the broad-based multi-disciplinary approach needed for RHIO.

- **Government.** Some government agencies exist to further RHIO-like purposes. Housing the RHIO entity in the government sector (either state or local) would likely serve to create a strong bond and working relationship with governmental healthcare service and benefits providers that may be integral to implementation of a successful RHIO strategy and that may not be in a position to be so engaged absent government sponsorship of the RHIO. However, government agencies may not be able to support critical business planning and implementation. Due to competing demands, budget limitations, system-wide resistance to risk-taking, and limited flexibility and ability to respond rapidly to changing environments, the government sector may not be viewed as the ideal environment for incubating and maturing a RHIO.

- **Non-profit Community Organizations.** Many non-profit community organizations exist for the advance of healthcare in their regions. For example, community councils that are formed and operated to promote health and prevent disease, especially among those at greatest risk, through education, outreach and advocacy will also embody the purposes underlying the desire to establish a RHIO. These organizations may involve the broad range of stakeholders who would be drawn to the formation of a RHIO serving the same geographic area as the existing non-profit organization. In addition, the non-profit organizations could potentially bring instant credibility to the startup RHIO activities, as well as infrastructure and financial resources.

Incubators

In order to mitigate some of the disadvantages associated with creating a new entity, a phased approach can be taken to developing the new entity. Effectively initiating this new, start-up enterprise is just as important as reaching the milestones and targets that

Table 2-1. Existing vs. New Entity: Advantages and Disadvantages

Structure	Advantages	Disadvantages
Use an existing entity	• Stable, well respected entity can potentially ease the transition from planning to operations and gain broader and more immediate acceptance • More cost effective, because certain start-up costs and inefficiencies can be avoided or minimized • Less time intensive than creating a new organization • May already be recognized as tax-exempt • Established relationships and history of collaboration • Established communication mechanisms	• May be unable to identify an existing entity that is neutral and not biased towards its existing mission • May not be perceived as being a neutral party • RHIO may not receive full attention if subsumed by an existing organization • May not have appropriate broad based representation within organization or its board • No existing organization does what RHIO contemplates doing
Create a new entity	• Neutrality of a new organization developed solely to fulfill RHIO's mission • Can ensure appropriate representation among membership and board • Can be phased in over time in an appropriate manner • If new entity is outside government, can be insulated from direct political intervention	• Higher infrastructure costs related to creation of a new entity • New organization has little to no credibility and visibility • May spend an inordinate amount of time raising funds to support its existence • Amount of resources used developing a new governing body • Securing recognition of tax-exemption may be time-consuming and costly

are specific to the RHIO. Particularly if the RHIO business plan requires a full-service launch in order to be successful, all elements of the workforce, facilities, infra-structure and support system must be in place at a single point in time. Acquisition of these elements in that context is always costly, difficult and inefficient. Instead of initiating a full-service launch of the RHIO entity, the RHIO organizers can engage a nonprofit incubator by contract to provide the workforce, facilities, infrastructure and support incrementally as required. The transitional approach calls for the development of a RHIO program office within the incubator. Once the RHIO entity is organized and its tax-exempt status recognized, it would be in a position to assume the assets and liabilities of the program office.

Virtual Entities

Does the RHIO really need to be housed in an entity at all, or can it be virtual, that is, a creature of executory contracts among the necessary stakeholders? A virtual entity may be appropriate to carry out RHIO purposes and functions by agreement of key stakeholders who mutually agree to do so through contract. This would be similar in many respects to a limited liability company or partnership, except that a new entity is not formed to become the RHIO and one or more contracting stakeholders (collectively "Lead Stakeholder") would undertake to perform RHIO functions, with the support, through decision-making, funding and in-kind participation of other stakeholders. State and regional data reporting consortia are often structured in this way.

The virtual entity is a model similar to the incubator model, except that the RHIO would not transition away from the incubator but would continue to operate in that manner for a specific period or term of contract. The stakeholders or RHIO members would empower the Lead Stakeholder to act on their behalf, subject to some oversight, in implementing and managing RHIO functions. This empowerment could be accomplished through mutual powers of attorney that confer upon the Lead Stakeholder the authority to bind all stakeholders to the extent specified in the powers of attorney themselves.

Form of Entity Assessment Tool

During the planning process, it should become reasonably evident that two or three or possibly more of the models are likely candidates as the appropriate form of entity for the RHIO. Assessment tools, like the one in Appendix C: Matrix of Entity and Governance Objectives and Principles Matched to Organization Options, can help stakeholders identify preferred entity and governance objectives and principles.

RHIO Governance Roles and Responsibilities

The governance structure of an organization is set forth in bylaws of a corporation, in the operating agreement of a limited liability company, the partnership agreement of a partnership, the enabling legislation of a public body, or the contracts among stakeholders in a virtual entity. The formal governance structure should reflect the decisions that were made earlier with respect to establishing governance principles. Regardless of the form of entity and the corresponding governance documentation, the particulars of governance are usually broken down as follows:

- Where the principal locations for the conduct of business will be, including whether meetings shall be conducted;
- The fiscal year of the organization, which effectively sets the organization's calendar for actions by members or shareholders, nomination and election of governing board members, annual reporting, the audit cycle, and other governance related functions;
- Identity or qualifications of stakeholders and specification of their rights as such, including voting, access to records, receipt of reports and, in organizations that are not nonprofit, the rights to participate in distributions of profits;
- Powers of governing body members, which are generally very broad and rarely circumscribed by the overarching powers of stakeholders;
- Duties of governing board members, including fiduciary duties owed to the organization;
- Number and qualifications of governing board members;
- Limitations on who can serve as governing board members (e.g., many states provide that for nonprofit organizations, only a certain percentage of governing

board members may be "interested," i.e., be compensated by the organization for services);

- Manner of election and appointment of board members, terms of office, how vacancies are filled, how governing board members may be removed or resign;
- The particulars of governing board meetings, including quorum requirements, frequency, how notices are given, and how board actions may be taken without a meeting;
- Governing board member compensation and reimbursement;
- Establishment of standing committees of the board, such as executive, compensation, governance, audit and finance committees, and specification of their powers and particulars as to meetings;
- Establishment of advisory committees, including, for example, a steering committee of key stakeholders, a policy committee providing guidance regarding development, enhancement and implementation of RHIO programs, and an interoperability committee providing guidance regarding system functionality and participant connectivity;
- Designation and responsibilities of officers; and
- Maintenance of records and reporting obligations to stakeholders, constituents, and governmental oversight agencies.

Addressing Conflicts of Interest

An important element of the success of a RHIO will be its ability to transact business transparently and with apparent fairness to all RHIO constituencies. One aspect of transparency is the manner in which the RHIO will address conflicts of interest, real and perceived, in transactions between those in a position to influence RHIO decision-making and the RHIO itself. Because RHIO constituents are expected to have relationships with each other and with others with whom the RHIO will be conducting business, a legally sound and practical approach to addressing conflicts of interest should be adopted.

Generally speaking, the statutory and regulatory provisions of each state that govern the establishment of legal entities will contain specific provisions regarding conflicts of interest. This is particularly true for corporations, both for-profit and nonprofit. In addition, for entities that are recognized as tax-exempt, the prohibitions against self-dealing, so-called "Excess Benefits Transactions" and private benefit and inurement under federal and state tax laws, impose specific requirements for addressing conflicts of interest.

It is advisable that a formal conflicts of interest policy be adopted by the RHIO governing body. This policy should include rules for addressing conflicts of interest and also should include practical procedures for routine disclosure by interested parties to aid in the identification of potential conflicts of interest. A sound conflicts of interest policy should contain the following 11 elements:

- Statement as to the rationale for the policy, including its basis in law;
- General guidelines for conduct of governing body members and officers (e.g., confidentiality, loyalty, duty of care);

- Definition of when a conflict of interest exists (e.g., when the RHIO proposes to enter into a transaction with a person who has a financial interest in the transaction and is in a position to influence RHIO decision-making);
- Identification of those persons considered to be in a position to influence RHIO decision-making (e.g., directors, officers and their immediate family members);
- What constitutes a financial interest in a transaction that could give rise to a conflict of interest (e.g., direct or indirect interests in the non-RHIO party to the transaction);
- Specific instances where a conflict of interest is deemed to exist and measures to insulate the RHIO from the potential influence of an interested person (e.g., officers shall not vote on matters pertaining to his or her compensation);
- Procedures for disclosing actual or potential conflicts of interest and for determining if in fact a conflict of interest exists;
- Procedures for acting on a transaction in which a person in a position to influence decision-making has a financial interest;
- Special procedures for addressing Excess Benefit Transactions under the Internal Revenue Code and regulations;
- Procedures for addressing violations of the conflicts of interest policy; and
- Form of interested party questionnaire to be completed and reviewed at least annually.

Tax Considerations for RHIOs

Section 501(c)(3) Charitable Organization Status

Organizations that are organized and operated primarily for charitable and/or public purposes may seek exemption under section 501(c)(3) of the Internal Revenue Code and parallel provisions of state laws governing exemptions from state corporate income or franchise tax. These laws offer tax exemption and enable contributors to take an income tax deduction for charitable donations they make to the organization. In general, section 501(c)(3) organizations may freely receive grants from other section 501(c)(3) organizations or a section 501(c)(4) organization (described below). Section 501(c)(3) organizations may not engage in any political campaign activities. Such organizations are permitted to advocate and attempt to influence legislation, provided they do not devote a substantial part of their activities to lobbying.

Section 509(a)(2) Public Charity Status

Within the section 501(c)(3) classification, there are two distinct categories of organizations: "public charities" and "private foundations." A section 501(c)(3) organization is presumed to be a private foundation unless it can demonstrate that it meets one of the tests for qualification as a public charity. Private foundations are subject to a number of excise taxes and restrictions on their activities that do not apply to public charities. In addition, gifts to private foundations generally are deductible by donors at lower thresholds than gifts to public charities. Private foundations are also subject to more burdensome and time-consuming recordkeeping and reporting requirements. Accordingly, classification as a public charity is in almost all cases more favorable than classification as a private foundation.

One way for a section 501(c)(3) organization to qualify as a public charity is to meet the "one third/one third test" under section 509(a)(2). In order to meet the one test, the organization must receive more than one third of its support from a combination of gifts and fees from its exempt activities, and not more than one third of its support from investment income. All contributions from "substantial contributors" (persons or entities giving more than a certain amount relative to the organization's total support) are excluded in calculating support from gifts. In addition, in computing the amount of support received from fees for exempt activities, fees received from any one person (including a governmental unit) are includable only to the extent that they do not exceed the greater of $5,000 or 1% of the organization's total support for the year. Thus, it can be difficult for an organization to meet the one third/one third test if it receives major gifts from substantial contributors or fees for exempt activities from only a limited number of payors who are subject to the $5,000/1% limitation.

Section 501(c)(4) Social Welfare Organization

Organizations that are organized and operated primarily for social welfare purposes may seek exemption under section 501(c)(4) of the Internal Revenue Code and parallel provisions of state laws. Section 501(c)(4) organizations generally face more restrictions on funding sources than do section 501(c)(3) organizations. Unlike with section 501(c)(3) organizations, donors to section 501(c)(4) organizations are not entitled to take a charitable income tax deduction for contributions, and donations to section 501(c)(4) organizations may even be subject to a gift tax. In addition, it is generally more difficult and disadvantageous for section 501(c)(3) private foundations to make grants to section 501(c)(4) organizations. It can also be difficult for section 501(c)(3) public charities to make grants to section 501(c)(4) organizations, further limiting a section 501(c)(4) organization's ability to attract support for operations. Unlike section 501(c)(3) organizations, however, section 501(c)(4) organizations may take a position in support of or in opposition to a candidate for public office, provided this type of political activity is not its primary purpose. In addition, section 501(c)(4) organizations can engage in unlimited lobbying activities, provided such activities are relevant to and further the organization's exempt purposes.

Section 501(c)(6) Business League Status

Organizations formed by persons having a common business interest and organized and operated to promote that common business interest may seek exemption from federal corporate income tax under section 501(c)(6) of the Internal Revenue Code, and under parallel sections of state law. In order to qualify for tax-exemption as a section 501(c)(6) organization, the organization must not be organized for profit, no part of its net earnings may inure to the benefit of any private shareholder or individual, and it must be devoted to improving business conditions of one or more lines of business. The organization may not engage in a regular business of the kind ordinarily carried on for profit. The organization's activities must promote common business interests in a way that is not simply performing particular services for specific persons such as its members, even if those services contribute to or are valuable for their businesses.

A section 501(c)(6) business league may promote legislation germane to a common business interest and may engage in lobbying on behalf of that common business interest. Lobbying may even be the organization's sole activity. Generally, a section 501(c)(6) organization may not be organized primarily to participate or intervene in political campaigns for or against candidates for public office, but may engage in some political activities.

Section 501(c)(3) public charities generally will be unable to make grants to a Section 501(c)(6) organization, and donors will not be entitled to deduct contributions to a Section 501(c)(6) organization as charitable donations. However, membership dues and other donations made by persons whose business interests are promoted by the Section 501(c)(6) organization may be deductible as business expenses.

For-Profit and Pass-Through Entities

A for-profit corporation generally is required to pay federal corporate income tax and, depending upon the laws of the states in which the corporation is organized and/or does business, to pay state income or franchise tax, property taxes, and other taxes.

General partnerships and their partners are separate entities for purposes of tax reporting; each must file the appropriate return. However, a general partnership and its partners are not separate entities for purposes of calculating or paying tax. The general partnership's income and losses flow through to its partners proportionately, and is taxed as income and loss to the partners individually. Generally, the same rules apply to limited partnerships and limited liability companies for federal income tax purposes, but may differ under certain states' laws.

Qualification of RHIO Entity as a Tax-Exempt Organization

Qualification as a Section 501(c)(3) Organization

The RHIO entity may be able to qualify as a Section 501(c)(3) organization on the basis that its activities promote and protect the health of the community. The RHIO entity also may be able to qualify as a Section 501(c)(3) organization on the basis that it lessens the burdens of government. For example, the RHIO entity may be able to qualify as a Section 501(c)(3) organization if it were to offer its services at substantially below cost (around 15% of the entity's cost of providing such services). In that situation, the RHIO entity may be required to seek grants from other organizations in addition to offering its services at substantially below cost in order to qualify as a charitable organization on this basis.

Qualification as a Section 501(c)(4) Organization

The RHIO entity may be able to qualify as a section 501(c)(4) organization on the basis that it promotes the common good and general welfare of the community and lessens the burdens of governments that are mandated by law to protect and improve the health of their residents and help ensure their access to medical care and treatment.

Qualification as a Section 501(c)(6) Organization

The RHIO entity may be able to qualify as a section 501(c)(6) organization on the basis that its activities promote the common business interests of healthcare providers and/or payors by facilitating electronic health information exchange. Section 501(c)(6) status would not permit the organization simply to operate an information exchange, but would permit it to promote such an exchange in a variety of ways, including lobbying, development of standard contracting practices and other measures, facilitating dealings between RHIO participants and vendors, and so on.

Supporting IT Procurement with an Effective Governance Structure

Software and IT equipment procurement is a complicated process that requires a high level of effort and commitment by the RHIO's governing body and executive management. Given the multiplicity of products from which to choose and the catastrophic consequences that can result from implementation failure, management must play an active role in IT procurement to ensure proper selection and successful implementation of the products.

For any major procurement effort, a procurement team should be established to be responsible for the project from start to finish. This team should consist of at least one member from the RHIO's governing body, such as the Chief Information Officer (CIO) or Chief Technology Officer (CTO), who will have high level oversight of and champion the project, hold others accountable, bring to bear the resources necessary to ensure the project's success, and make the final procurement decisions for the RHIO. The rest of the team should be staffed by another high-level member of the organization's IT department to manage the day-to-day aspects of the project, as well as two end users who can provide "real world" feedback and input regarding their needs. Finally, consider hiring a third-party IT consultant with expertise in the technology to be procured. This person can provide invaluable guidance and advice with respect to the project. Each of these team members should report to the CIO or CTO, who in turn will report to executive management on procurement issues, at every critical stage of the procurement project.

Once the procurement team is appointed, a smaller working group should be formed from the team to determine the RHIO's technology needs and analyze the extent what specifically needs to be purchased. This group should include the IT department member, at least one end user, and the third party consultant. The working group should conduct a requirements analysis of the RHIO's critical technology needs, as well as those that are not essential but that would be useful tools. Included in this evaluation must be a risk analysis that at a minimum addresses HIPAA requirements. The results of the assessment should be reported to the procurement team and the CIO/CTO, who in turn would present the report to the RHIO's executive management team, so that final decisions may be made concerning what software and IT hardware should be procured.

After the needs are assessed, a procurement budget must be established. For substantial purchases, the CFO and others in the accounting department should interface with the working group and the procurement team as a whole to balance the RHIO's procurement needs with any budget constraints.

Once the budget is prepared, the working group should investigate the various product options in the market. The third-party expert must play a major role in this process and should be able to compare the RHIO's requirements with the products being considered to determine if they possess the necessary functions and features. The procurement team also should consider whether a request for proposal specifying the RHIO's technical and functional requirements should be issued, which would be prepared by the working group. The entire procurement team should evaluate the responses to the RFP and view live demonstrations from the prospective vendors, rank the options in order of preference, and explain its recommendation to the RHIO's executive management regarding the desired choice.

When the choice of products has been made, the RHIO then must negotiate the contract with the vendor. At this point, engagement of legal counsel, either in-house or an outside lawyer, with relevant technology procurement experience is essential. This lawyer should interface with the CIO/CTO and the third party consultant to ensure he/she understands the RHIO's critical needs, desires, and constraints. An attorney experienced in negotiating procurement contracts will be able to ensure that all of these issues are addressed in the contract and also will help the RHIO avoid or at least minimize disputes in the future. Once the contract is negotiated but before it is executed, it should be reviewed by the procurement team to address any unforeseen or unanticipated issues, and then be presented to RHIO executive management for approval.

After the products have been purchased, a separate team must be formed to implement the technology. The members of the procurement team may be used, but they must be supplemented with others from the IT department having the technical expertise necessary to assist the vendor in the installation of the products, conversion of the RHIO's legacy data, and testing of the products before they go live. A project manager, who is a member of this team, also should be appointed to take a leadership role in this stage of the procurement. Ideally, the project manager would be the IT person who was part of the procurement team. The implementation team also should remain in place after installation in order to monitor the ongoing use of the software and IT products and report to interface with the vendor and report to management in the event problems arise. Management's role in the implementation and monitoring phases is minimal, other than to select the implementation team and receive regular status reports.

CHAPTER 3

RHIO Evaluation and Sustainability

Beth Friedmann, Jeffrey P. Holmes, Todd Frech,
Keith MacDonald, and Laura Kolkman

Why Start with Evaluation?

When planning a RHIO, it is easy to fall into the trap of good intentions. Calls for health information exchange by state and federal officials reinforce the notion that RHIOs play a significant role in reducing medical errors and improving quality of care. It is a noble undertaking. However, the challenge is to define and actually measure quality. Even if medical errors are reduced after implementing a RHIO, can it be said with certainty that the RHIO was the cause? Is it possible that other quality initiatives contributed to the change?

Evaluation is often associated with the end of a project. It is commonly looked at as part of the "wrap up"; after all, what is there to evaluate before the work is actually completed? In fact, the opposite is true: Evaluation is not a task, but a process! The evaluation process must be initiated at the early stages of RHIO planning. It is at this juncture that stakeholders define the goals of their organization, and so it is at this point that stakeholders must also determine how they will measure success and be satisfied that their goals have been met. Meeting goals and expectations of key stakeholders and knowing to whom various benefits accrue is crucial to long-term sustainability,

Consideration must also be given to how RHIO stakeholders align financial goals with quality of care. If sharing data leads to reduced laboratory tests, does this then lead to ultimately decreased revenues for a provider? Does an evaluation that demonstrates quality accompanied by lost revenues qualify as a success? This scenario points out the need to balance the accrual of benefits from the various viewpoints.

The challenge of any evaluation is to define and measure quality from the stakeholder's perspective. Part of meeting that challenge is to understand who the stakeholders are and to realize they may not be only the people or organizations that provide financial or technical support for the RHIO. They are also members of the community and consumers of healthcare. As a result, it is critical in this type of community project to understand how the public views the benefits and success of the RHIO. Without broad public support from *the patients* who will be served by the RHIO, the project will fail. If the public and consumers of healthcare services do not see the benefit, then other stakeholders that are critical for success—hospitals, physician offices, and laboratories—will hesitate to participate.

Evaluation is a complex undertaking, and from the outset of a RHIO project, shared common goals and each stakeholder's vision of success must be clear. Any misalignment of goals must be identified and resolved to the satisfaction of all stakeholders. This is especially true when facing the decision for selecting the business model to ensure sustainability, because RHIOs may appear successful in the early stages of development, during which time they are likely to be funded by grants. However, the transition to long-term sustainability implies a different set of requirements, because financing will be derived from sources with varied business goals.

Demonstrating Value

Regardless of the strategy, financial support and success of a RHIO is predicated on the ability of the organization to demonstrate value. This value may be defined differently by the various stakeholders and at times the definitions may be at odds with each other.

Payors may look for results that are consistent with pay-for-performance objectives such as reduction in complications suffered by patients with chronic diseases. Hospitals may be attracted to the concept of a true community-wide paperless record and the reduction in paper process and associated manual costs. Private practitioners may find value in efficiencies that are gained in having a more complete view of the patient's medical history, the ability to electronically exchange information with other providers, and the efficiencies gained in eliminating much of the manual management of a paper-based health record.

Stakeholders are skeptical of promises and the good intentions of RHIOs, because the healthcare industry is rife with stories of failed IT projects. The proof, therefore, must be in the numbers—concrete data that drive strategic and financial decisions and ultimately the RHIO's viability. Thus, in planning for long-term sustainability it is essential to have an evaluation process with solid metrics, however success is defined.

In light of these considerations, listed here are some initial questions that RHIOs will want to consider as they begin the evaluation process:

- To whom is the evaluation targeted (stakeholders, the community)?
- What are the goals of the various stakeholder groups?
- Are the definitions and objectives within those goals clear? If not, who will define them? How will they be measured?
- Will there be a committee assigned to the evaluation process, or will an outside organization be engaged?
- How will the evaluation committee's neutrality be ensured?
- How does each stakeholder measure success or define return on investment (ROI)?
- What types of evaluation are needed to secure funding?

Practical Issues

There are a host of tools available to utilize in the evaluation process—many of which can be adapted to the clinical environment. Investigators or project managers can, for example, organize focus groups with employees to elicit their reactions to their use of technology, or to the goals of the RHIO overall. Income and expense reports may document cost savings. Time to disposition, measures of crowding in emergency departments, changes in admission patterns, utilization, and consumer satisfaction are just a few of the other valuable measures that can be applied to the question: "Was the RHIO successful?"

Given the many questions and varied approaches to answering them, it may be difficult to know where to begin. A good starting point may revolve around the practicality and cost involved in implementing a given evaluation plan. In this case the questions to be considered are:

- Who is responsible for initiating the evaluation?
- What *specific* question (or questions) will the evaluation answer?
- What's the easiest way to answer the question(s)?
- How valuable is it to know the answer to that question (nice to know vs. must know)?
- What type of resources (human and financial) will be required to implement the evaluation tool?
- How reliable is the tool?
- How long will it take to complete the study (and will it be completed in time to secure long-term funding)?
- Is the study disruptive to workflow?
- Are there issues relating to HIPAA or clinical subject research that must be resolved?
- Are the evaluators experienced and sufficiently objective so as to guarantee the validity of the results?
- What are the barriers to implementing the evaluation?
- Will the evaluation be applicable across participating organizations, and if not, how will this affect the usefulness of the results?
- When is the evaluation needed?

Putting It All Together in an Evaluation Plan

As with all complex tasks, the answers to these and many more detailed questions should be organized into an action plan. At the early stages of the RHIO, an evaluation plan demonstrates to all stakeholders that the project is being carefully managed and that the RHIO is putting into place mechanisms to ensure accountability. The plan should include timelines for implementation, resource requirements, study design specifications for various efforts and clearly defined deliverables.

For detailed examples of measures that can be used to evaluate IT projects, visit the Agency for Healthcare Research and Quality (AHRQ) Evaluation Toolkit Web site.[1]

Financial Metrics

In many communities healthcare organizations compete for healthcare dollars. In such a competitive atmosphere, organizations may hesitate to release key competitive indicators that would otherwise be useful in quantifying the RHIO's success. If all the RHIO's members can agree to share evaluation information such as financial metrics early in the planning process, then it is much easier to conduct a useful evaluation of the RHIO's success. Securing agreement among all members must be one of the first and most important points of negotiation during the formation of the RHIO.

Of course, information that members share for the purposes of evaluation must be kept confidential. Organizations may choose to leave the evaluation process to a third party that will provide only consolidated information rather than data that may be tracked to an individual organization. The RHIO may choose to allow members to veto the release of information they feel may be detrimental to their ability to remain competitive in the community. In whatever way the RHIO chooses to accomplish this task, it is important that as much information as possible be available to support an evaluation that will point to success and sustainability.

One frequently discussed benefit of a RHIO is the potential for cost savings. These costs savings can be hard, meaning that direct savings can be quantified and a dollar amount can be calculated, or they can be soft, meaning that the savings are difficult to quantify and that a specific dollar amount cannot be directly calculated. In order to be successful, an evaluation must calculate the hard cost savings, convert soft to hard costs whenever possible, and clearly delineate the soft cost savings a RHIO achieves. Even more importantly, understanding how various members of the RHIO will consider the results of these evaluations is critical to the effort of developing sustainability.

Increased efficiency is an example of soft cost savings produced by RHIOs especially for those forming with the goal of making data exchange more efficient among RHIO members. Evaluating the benefits of increased efficiency of data exchange can be challenging and requires the cooperation of a wide variety of members. These benefits may seem obvious, but the benefits will remain unrealized unless the efficiencies are implemented properly and organizations actually take advantage of them.

If the efficiency gains are available but organizations do not take advantage of them, these "unrealized benefits" will make it difficult to demonstrate the success of the RHIO. For example, if a RHIO member participates in data exchange that increases efficiencies and would allow the participant to reduce staffing, but that staffing reduction is not actually taken, then the benefits are potential, and not realized. A successful evaluation must identify these benefits and present the potential benefits compared to the actual benefits.

While some soft cost savings are difficult to measure, others can easily be converted into hard financial metrics. For example, a RHIO could quantify its success with reducing emergency department bed turnaround time by demonstrating that decreases achieved resulted in the opportunity for X number of additional patients per day to be seen, which translates into dollars of additional revenue.

Depending on how a RHIO is structured and the services it offers, there may be many different benefits available to the RHIO members. To create evaluation tools that will demonstrate the benefits and encourage their widest possible realization a great deal of cooperation among members is required. Some members may need assistance to implement the system's capabilities in a way that achieves the maximum benefit. For example, having access to a standard formulary might provide some cost savings for health plans and for patients who are required to pay for medications that are not on the formulary. Obvious benefits to both payors and patients could be demonstrated if the central formulary was available to the RHIO in a way that would automatically update systems with the appropriate medications when they are available. This particular benefit, while potentially large and impacting both payors and patients, may not be easily implemented by smaller providers without assistance.

Designing effective evaluation tools requires an intimate knowledge of healthcare operations, access to data, and the ability to define the program's success in accordance with its unique features.

A successful evaluation program will be customized to the specifics of a RHIO's operation. This section discusses some potential evaluations that may be applied to many different RHIO programs.

Financial Management

RHIOs that are interested in demonstrating financial benefits may want to consider evaluating some or all of the elements shown in Table 3-1.

Table 3-1. Financial Management Measures and Potential Benefits

Measurement	Potential Benefits
Delay in claim payments that are held pending a request for additional information or for incomplete information	More efficient access to information may reduce the total number of hours associated with fulfilling requests for additional information.
	Faster response to requests for additional information will reduce delays in claim payments and improve the organization's cash flow.
Percentage of rejected claims	Decreasing the percentage of rejected claims increases cash flow and decreases the percentage of claims that cannot be paid due to delays in submission.
Time between the delivery of service and the receipt of payment	By reducing the amount of time that elapses between the delivery of service and the receipt of payment, cash flow is increased, and the percentage of claims that are delayed due to missing or incomplete information is reduced.
Reduction in unnecessary hospitalizations	More complete health information in the hands of the primary care, emergency staff and consulting physicians may reduce admissions that are related to an incomplete view of the patient's condition.
More accurate identification of community health needs	Understanding the health of the community as a whole will allow communities to target their healthcare dollars to programs that can have the greatest impact.

Benefits Associated with More Efficient Use of Personnel

Many IT initiatives are sold on the promise of reductions in administrative and operational costs. This can be difficult to measure; understanding the cost savings requires a detailed knowledge of how an organization operates, and the organization must be prepared to implement the steps that will fully realize the cost savings. Cost savings often provide a business case for IT expenditures but are unrealized when the organization does not actually follow through with staff reductions, personnel reassignments or reorganization of the organization's workflow. It is often the case that the work that needs to be done to realize the benefits of an IT program is costly in itself. Table 3-2 presents some measurements a RHIO may put in place in order to characterize benefits associated with efficient use of personnel.

Workflow Management

Efficiency can also be recognized through better access to a patient's problem list, allergy list, medication list, and lab data, which would otherwise have required a phone call. Examples of these metrics are shown in Table 3-3.

Clinical Care Measures

Clinical care measures are often difficult to associate with hard cost savings because the ability to document clinical outcomes, which would indicate potential cost savings, is still a challenge for many organizations. In cases where organizations have programs in place to identify clinical outcomes, the data from these programs can be used to evaluate and show potential outcomes that will support sustainability. Examples of these metrics are shown in Table 3-4.

In addition, for many RHIOs achieving measurably improved patient outcomes across the community is the ultimate goal. As a result, these clinical care measures can be incorporated into quality improvement activities focused on initiatives for:
- Reducing adverse drug events (ADEs);
- Reducing patient mortality;

Table 3-2. Personnel Use Measures and Potential Benefits

Measurement	Potential Benefit
Number of staff members needed to support partner organizations	Salary and benefits make up one of the largest costs for any organization. A reduction in staffing will have a significant and rapid effect on an organization's revenue.
Number of visits each licensed provider can accommodate	Increasing patient visits without the addition of staff will have an immediate impact on revenue. The revenue benefit can often be supported without changes to the existing support infrastructure.
Decrease in the need for the storage and retrieval of health records from the local hospital or IDN	Online access to the patient's health information will reduce the need to have charts pulled and copied or delivered for patients being seen in the physician's office, clinics, or during hospitalizations.

Table 3-3. Workflow Management Measures and Potential Benefits

Measurement	Potential Benefit
Reduction in the number of staff members needed to support the delivery of patient care (physician office or inpatient setting)	Automating and sharing information can reduce the number of support personnel needed to provide care for a patient.
Reduction in duplicate orders	Often it is easier (and faster) if a physician reorders a test instead of waiting to have the information located and delivered.
Reduction in patient wait times in office or stays in hospital settings	Reduction in wait times for patients who have been seen in a physician's office, emergency departments, or even in an inpatient setting to have their information located and reviewed by their primary care provider.
Reduction in medication administration errors	Access to a complete medication list can reduce the potential for overdoses when patients see multiple care providers and cannot verbalize the medications they are currently taking.
Increased patient satisfaction levels	The decrease in patient dissatisfaction with long wait times while critical information is located, or by additional needle sticks or uncomfortable repeat procedures, can be significant.

- Reducing admissions and re-admissions; and
- Compliance with American Medical Association (AMA), Centers for Medicare & Medicaid Services (CMS), Health Plan Employer Data Information Set (HEDIS), or other clinical measures.

Utilization Management

Increased availability of patient information across a community (including active diagnoses, test results, medication history, and patient-specific formularies) can also lead to improved utilization of services for patients, as measured by:

- Average number of inpatient admissions per patient and percentage of readmissions;
- Average inpatient lengths-of-stay;
- Average number of emergency department visits per patient;
- Average number of ambulatory visits per patient;
- Pharmacy expenses:
  - Number of prescriptions per patient
  - Average per-prescription costs
  - Number or cost of prescriptions written off-formulary; and
- Duplicate inpatient and ambulatory laboratory, radiology, and other imaging tests.

User Satisfaction

Among the many factors contributing to the failure of healthcare IT projects, one of the most confounding revolves around user satisfaction. A project can be technically

Table 3-4. Measures of Clinical Care and Potential Benefits

Measurement	Potential Benefit
Duplicate testing performed by providers	A reduction of duplicate testing also has a clinical benefit. Not exposing patients to additional discomfort or delays in treatment while waiting for testing is a clear benefit and will certainly improve patient satisfaction and possibly consumer loyalty.
Treatment programs for complex patients—chronic disease management	Coordination of care for patients who are seeing multiple specialists or who are enrolled in a case management program can be difficult if the patients' medical information is difficult to obtain. The benefits of more closely monitoring these patients include potentially preventing admissions and complications or reducing the disruption to their daily activities.
Response to patient inquiries such as prescription refills, referral requests, and other types of medical-administrative processes	Primary care providers often do not have the complete picture of patients who have multiple specialists, and it can be difficult to route patients through complex approval processes. This results in increased workload for administrative staff and delays in care and requires more time from administrative staff to arrange these services.
Community-based healthcare resource planning	Identifying needed programs and more importantly the success of these programs in the community is a huge challenge to most communities. RHIOs potentially have access to aggregate information, which will help facilitate community-wide health assessments and identify utilization trends.
Disease surveillance/registry	Public health departments are often interested in the capabilities of RHIOs because the information that is collected could potentially provide a detailed snapshot of a community's health and allow rapid response in disease outbreaks or other emergencies.

sound. It can meet all of its functional specifications and yet, if it is perceived by users to be unfriendly or cumbersome, the entire project is shelved. While technology is not the only element determining success or failures of a RHIO, it plays an important role. Thus, user satisfaction with the technology is of paramount importance when planning a RHIO.

Factors that influence user satisfaction fall into two general categories: usability and usefulness. Users will not embrace a system that is difficult to learn or tedious to use. Further, a system that is easy to use, but is perceived not to provide value, will likely fail as well.

For example, if an emergency department attempts to implement data exchange, without the participation of primary care providers, medication information may be incomplete or inaccurate. Frequent gaps in the data will result in user dissatisfaction and likely result in a poor adoption rate of the technology. This will then lower the success rate for RHIO implementation. Therefore, perceived—and real—reliability of data, particularly when it forms the basis for clinical decisions, is a key factor and should be measured.

Usability as a Factor in User Satisfaction

It cannot be emphasized enough that the evaluation process as it relates to technology begins at the early stages of design. Testing user satisfaction solely at the end of a project is inadequate. This approach often results in low adoption rates and budget overruns. Costs associated with fixing problems after rollout are extremely high as compared with resolution of user issues during development. These costs combined with lost support among users can derail a project.

Interestingly, although the risk of designing systems without ongoing input from users is well known, this area continues to be overlooked. Perhaps this is because user testing is time consuming, as it requires participation by actual users.

Approaches to user acceptance testing include:
- Surveys to identify clinical and workflow concerns of users;
- Heuristic evaluation;
- Use case analysis; and
- Focus groups.

In addition, evaluation after implementation should determine the frequency with which data made available by the RHIO is actually accessed. This can be determined through system logs and workflow observation. If it is determined that particular data elements are used infrequently, focus groups can help to explain whether the data shared is perceived to be of limited value or whether the method of delivery is unsatisfactory.

User testing can be disruptive to workflow and requires that coverage be arranged while evaluation takes place. Many project managers rely on the vendor or designer, whom they assume has the experience and knowledge to anticipate user needs. This is an erroneous assumption and can result in system problems that are quite expensive.

It is worth noting that frequently when users are asked to list functions they would like a system to perform, they describe tasks in general terms. Users tend to be less knowledgeable about how these tasks should be accomplished. It is not uncommon for a user testing a system to realize that the functionality they thought would be useful, in fact, is not.

To address this issue in a timely fashion, designers sometimes employ a technique known as rapid prototyping. The user is asked to test a system multiple times in its rough form, early in the design process. User input elicited at this juncture and throughout development increases the likelihood that users will embrace a new system. Changes at this stage are also less expensive to implement. Usability software can be used to help to identify user problems during both development and rollout.

Usefulness as a Factor in User Satisfaction

Usefulness addresses issues related to the perceived value of a data sharing initiative. Evaluation of usefulness asks questions such as:

- Do you find that data retrieved through the RHIO initiative enhances the quality of care for your patients?
- Are you more efficient in your work as a result of the data access the RHIO provides?
- Do you believe the results of a RHIO search are reliable?
- Do you have adequate access to the RHIO information you need (sufficient number of workstations, convenient location, etc)?
- Is the cost of the RHIO outweighed by the benefits it offers?

Focus groups, satisfaction surveys and observation are all effective ways of evaluating user perceptions of a RHIO's utility and value. The examples that follow are a sample of the types of barriers identified using these techniques in existing health information exchange initiatives:

- Data is accessed and printed but misfiled in the chart.
- Providers are made aware of RHIO data too late to be of value (i.e., to prevent unnecessary tests).
- Provider usage is low because they are expected to remember multiple passwords to access multiple systems.
- Consumer-targeted sites are written using too much medical jargon.
- Providers are concerned about the accuracy of patient matching.
- Relevance of the information return to providers or consumers is not certain.

RHIOs are, for the most part, relatively young. As such, evaluation techniques for these types of initiatives are still evolving. As more and more RHIOs face the challenge of sustainability, documenting value through careful evaluation will play an increasingly important role in securing the resources necessary for long term success.

Developing a Sustainable Business Model: Securing Initial Funding

Many businesses need a financial benefactor to support initial operations. For RHIOs today, that often means one or more grants or gifts. Federal and state agencies, foundations, and philanthropic organizations are common sources of grants for RHIOs. RHIO founding members often provide start-up assistance with both cash and in-kind contributions. In addition, a number of major corporations including payor organizations have provided start-up funds and assistance. These grants and gifts provide the RHIO time to establish its business value and position itself for business sustainability. Initially, however, the RHIO is dependent upon the gifts and grants of interested parties and organizations. Some options in funding source types include the following (see also Table 3-5).

Government Grants: Federal, State, and Local

Government grants have been made available to RHIOs and other entities for the purposes of testing electronic medical record (EMR) adoption, defining governance structures, developing healthcare information exchange (HIE) infrastructure, testing data exchange, and related HIE activities. To apply, applicants must typically complete a request for proposal (RFP) and either partner with or act as a "prime" contractor for the grant. The specifics for each type of grant can be found on the respective Web sites.

Table 3-5. Resource Directory for Grants and Start-up Funding

Organization	Type of information	Web site
Office of National Health Information Technology Coordinator	Information on research, current priorities, and federal programs focused on HIT, including funding opportunities	http://www.hhs.gov/healthit/
Agency for Healthcare Research and Quality (AHRQ)	Information and research on HIT and patient safety issues; major federal funder of HIT projects	http://healthit.ahrq.gov/home/index.html
Centers for Medicare & Medicaid Services (CMS), Physician Focused Quality Initiative	Information on Quality Improvement Projects for providers • Pay for performance • Demo projects and evaluation reports • Opportunities for funding new "well developed and clearly thought out" projects that will improve quality and efficiency rather than providing more services	http://www.cms.hhs.gov
eHealth Initiative Foundation, Connecting Communities for Better Health, Resource Center	Information and research on community-based HIT projects around the country; plus sample resource documents	http://ccbh.ehealthinitiative.org/
Connecting for Health, Markle Foundation	Addressing barriers to development of an interconnected health information infrastructure through research, resource dissemination, and conferences	http://www.connectingforhealth.org/
Health eTechnologies Initiative, Robert Wood Johnson Foundation	Information on HIT research and provides funding opportunities	http://www.hetinitiative.org/
American Medical Informatics Association	Training healthcare professionals to serve as local informatics leaders and champions	http://www.amia.org/10x10/index.asp

Grants for HIE and RHIO activities have come from many sources. The following Web sites are sources for tracking open RFP solicitations:

- http://www.grants.gov/
- http://www.fedbizopps.gov/
- http://www.ahrq.gov/fund/
- http://toolkit.ehealthinitiative.org/value_creation_and_financing/resources.ms px?Section=384&Category=404&Document=607

Applicants must obtain a D & B Registration (DUNS® number) if applying for funding from federal government agencies. This can be obtained at: https://eupdate. dnb.com/requestOptions.html. There is no fee for obtaining a DUNS® number. Federal contracts will also require Central Contractor Registration (http://www.ccr.gov/), and a DUNS® number is required to complete this application.

Foundations and Philanthropic Organizations

Many foundations and philanthropic organizations are committed to HIE as a way to improve healthcare and reduce medical errors. These organizations issue RFPs for specific projects; many accept unsolicited proposals as well. A visit to their Web site will quickly reveal what the foundation's interests are and how to approach the foundation. A listing of these organizations can be found at www.guidestar.com. Notable healthcare IT-focused foundations include the following.

The Robert Wood Johnson Foundation

As the nation's largest philanthropy devoted to improving health and healthcare, RWJF supports training, education, research and projects that demonstrate effective ways to deliver health services, especially for the most vulnerable populations.

- http://www.rwjf.org/index.jsp
- http://www.rwjf.org/applications/whatwefund.jsp

    Preference is given to applicants that are public agencies or are tax-exempt under section 501(c)(3) of the Internal Revenue Code.

The eHealth Initiative: Connecting Communities for Better Health

Conducted by the eHealth Initiative in cooperation with the Department of Health and Human Services (HHS), this $11 million program is providing seed funding and technical support to state, regional, and community-based health information organizations and initiatives across the country.

- http://www.ehealthinitiative.org/
- http://ccbh.ehealthinitiative.org/communities/funded.mspx

    The eHealth Initiative Foundation is a partner in a collaboration led by the National Opinion Research Center (NORC) that includes the Center for Information Technology Leadership, Regenstrief Institute/Indiana University, Vanderbilt Center for Better Health, and the Computer Sciences Corporation, which is developing and operating the AHRQ National Resource Center for Health Information Technology, providing support to 108 AHRQ grantees/contracts, federal partners as well as the field in general.

The Markle Foundation

This foundation has sponsored many innovative and industry-leading projects that have resulted in new approaches to the use of information technology. Over the last few years, the Markle Foundation has been operating most of its own programs and has funded few unsolicited proposals. A foundation spokesperson noted, "We have found that the most effective way for us to leverage our resources is to structure and operate our own projects in cooperation with our partners instead of working as a traditional grant-making organization."

The Markle Foundation's approach involves convening multi-sectoral groups of leaders and innovators from technology, government, public interest organizations and business to bring about the technical and policy changes needed to enable breakthroughs in the public interest. They typically seek out partners to help achieve their goals. Currently their focus is on their health and national security programs.

- http://www.markle.org/markle_programs

The Markle Foundation's Connecting for Health was designed to address the challenges of mobilizing health information to improve quality, conduct timely research, empower patients to become full participants in their care, and bolster the public health infrastructure. All work developed by Connecting for Health is placed in the public domain.

RHIOs should not overlook local and regional community foundations and other philanthropic organizations. RHIO leaders are encouraged to explore local funding opportunities, especially if interested in matching grant opportunities, sometimes offered by national foundations, such as the ones identified above.

Provider and Provider-based Organizations

Hospitals, other healthcare organizations and professional associations often provide start-up funds and in-kind contributions of money, staff, facilities and equipment. The amounts and or formulas for such support have varied widely and can only be determined locally. These gifts may serve as the foundation for future annual membership fees and/or transaction and services fees.

Private Sector and Purchasers

Major employers, pharmaceutical corporations, and insurance companies have provided start-up funds as well as in-kind contributions including services, personnel, space and equipment. These early supporters may also become long-term funding participants as purchasers of services.

In the eHealth Initiative's Second Annual Survey of State, Regional, and Community-Based Health Information Exchanges and Organizations, 91% of those surveyed identified securing upfront funding as moderately or very difficult, and 84% identified developing a sustainable business model as moderately or very difficult.[2]

There are several reasons why RHIOs must move beyond initial grant and gift funding. High on that list is the fact that such funding sources are usually supporting what is important to them. The funding source has secured a vendor—the RHIO—to provide services of interest to or on behalf of the funding source. In the near term, this may benefit both the RHIO and the funding source but in the long term, the RHIO needs to demonstrate the agility to provide services that are aligned with and of value to its broader membership and service area. That means delivering and supporting services in an ongoing, self-sustainable way. In addition, it is clear that the winds of federal funding can change frequently and with these changes can come a redirection in project funding—for both the successes as well as the failures. In other words, federal funding can disappear.

While grants may play an ongoing role in funding the RHIO, such sources come at a high cost in terms of grant solicitation, planning and administration as well as business agility. Through time, a balance of revenue sources assures a more sustainable business model.

Sustainable Models beyond Initial Funding

One of the biggest challenges for RHIOs is sustaining them once initial start-up funding is exhausted. There are three key considerations related to sustainability for RHIOs: securing and maintaining a commitment from all stakeholders; defining a clear and compelling business case; and creating a revenue model that supports ongoing operations. Each of these elements is essential, and each has its own considerations that fledgling RHIOs should consider.

Sustaining Stakeholder Support

As addressed in Chapter 1, securing and maintaining stakeholder commitment requires a clear governance structure; strong, dedicated leadership from within the community; a clear and compelling vision with a roadmap for achieving it; and demonstrated, incremental progress towards that vision. RHIOs lacking any of these essential elements will have difficulty maintaining the interest and support of stakeholders.

While specific governance structures are discussed in Chapter 2, the intrinsic relationship between governance and sustainability cannot be overemphasized. Sustainability will come from a governance structure that involves stakeholders investing in and benefiting from the success of the RHIO, balances the needs of the diverse stakeholder groups, defines their equity in the project, and resolves concerns regarding ownership of and access to patient information.

The process of developing this structure requires a known and trusted community leader who has the respect of the RHIO stakeholders. Typically—though not always—this leader comes from a large health delivery organization within the community. Initially, the RHIO's lead position is usually a part-time volunteer representing an in-kind donation from one of the partnering organizations. However, as the RHIO matures, a dedicated leader in an executive role is necessary to sustain stakeholder support.

With an appropriate governance structure and a trusted leader in place, developing and maintaining a vision becomes the next essential requirement for gaining and ensuring continued stakeholder support. Developing this vision is a significant undertaking because it must describe a sufficiently clear and compelling ideal. One challenge in developing this vision is that it must appeal to a broad variety of interests and in the process achieve consensus among stakeholders who often have divergent objectives.

Maintaining stakeholder commitment, especially in the early stages, is essential to securing start-up funding and achieving the results necessary to generate adequate and sustainable contributions. Successful RHIOs will maintain continuous stakeholder commitment by demonstrating measurable progress towards their vision and communicating their success with milestones. This early success can be achieved by tackling smaller projects that rely on proven technologies, have short implementation timelines, and promise quick results in satisfying the needs of a few stakeholders. Interest and forward momentum among a *small* number of trading partners can sometimes be easier to achieve than getting *everyone* in the community to buy into one big project.

Early successes can also be achieved by focusing initial efforts on a small set of obtainable objectives and balancing these with the growth of the infrastructure. RHIOs that tackle a long list of initiatives without the necessary infrastructure in an effort to appease all stakeholders will require more resources and find making progress difficult. Incorporating plans for incremental initiatives in the vision can then help build and sustain secondary stakeholder interest along the way.

Building a Business Case

Securing commitment from all stakeholders often requires the development of a clear and compelling business case. Business cases can be developed once early stakeholder interest has been obtained and should describe in sufficient detail the importance of its vision and the value it expects to deliver in order to keep stakeholders engaged. Sound business cases include the following components:

- A compelling executive summary that engages potential stakeholders and sponsors;
- A short summary of the history, current status, and accomplishments of the organization;
- A clear description of the goals and objectives of the initiative, including a brief definition of the workflow changes and targeted information technology (or technologies) and examples of its successful implementation elsewhere;
- An overview of the likely clinical, financial and other benefits that this technology will produce based on published literature and other reliable sources;
- An estimate of the implementation costs based on the expected approach for the community;
- A calculation of the likely net benefits and to whom those benefits are expected to accrue; and
- The description of a model for ensuring the ongoing sustainability of the initiative.

In some cases, a brief discussion of the risks and challenges associated with the implementation and use of the desired technology—including approaches for mitigating those risks—may be helpful or required.

Calculating costs requires a solid understanding of the implementation strategy for the initiative, including the estimated number of users over the course of the implementation period and into the production period. Cost estimates need to quantify as comprehensively as possible each of the components indicated in Table 3-6 that are appropriate for the planned implementation.

One of the most challenging components of a business case is calculating the benefits and determining to whom they will accrue. Presumably the desired or expected improvements will have been identified at the start of the effort. A potential list of benefits for a range of information technologies and the associated workflow changes is provided earlier in this chapter. The actual benefits *calculation* for the business case needs to consider the type of business model selected, the underlying technology required,

Table 3-6. Cost Estimates Needed for Initial and Ongoing Components

Initial Upfront Costs	Ongoing Costs
Hardware • Application and database servers • Network servers • User devices	Hardware • Ongoing maintenance fees and support
Software • Upfront license purchase costs, including any required third-party software	Software • Ongoing licensing costs
Personnel • Project management • Implementation resources, including clinical and training staff • Administrative support	Personnel • Ongoing implementation and support resources
Other • Office and other administrative expenses • Legal expenses • Consulting expenses • Marketing/communication • Travel	Other • Ongoing support resources • Evaluation expenses • Insurance

the extent to which the model and technology will be adapted in the community, and the types and nature of the payor/provider relationships in that community.

To whom these benefits accrue will vary by market. Depending on the level of capitation, risk contracts and pay-for-performance or pay-for-quality programs in place in that market, different stakeholders will experience different levels of benefit. For example, in markets with higher levels of capitation and delegated medical management, hospital networks and physician organizations will benefit to a larger extent than those in markets where payors and employers assume a larger share of the risk. These benefit calculations can be complicated, since each payor/employer and provider organization can have a distinct relationship—and even different levels of risk for different patient populations within those contracts.

Nonetheless, benefits calculations should address, where appropriate, the benefits for all of the following stakeholders:

- Hospitals and integrated delivery networks;
- Community clinics and safety net providers;
- Physician groups and practices;
- Nursing homes and long-term care facilities;
- Behavioral and mental health providers;
- Payors;
- Employers (both self-insured and non self-insured); and
- Patients.

Fortunately, increased acknowledgement of the benefits of sharing healthcare information has led some payors and employers to increase their support of some of those technologies enabling this capability.

Examples of payor-sponsored e-prescribing, electronic communication and e-visits between patients and physicians, and personal health records are becoming more prevalent. In many cases their funding supports the initial purchase and implementation of these technologies; in a few cases, payors are providing the ongoing support that will lead to long-term adoption and sustainability.

As described earlier in this chapter, measuring and quantifying value are essential if RHIOs are to gain and maintain support from stakeholders. As of the publication of this guide, few have successfully defined and demonstrated a model that has generated revenue and savings to cover ongoing costs.

Models for Revenue Generation

One important question that arises when establishing a RHIO is which business model for revenue generation to adopt to provide the foundation for financial sustainability. Because business models are inextricably linked to financial sustainability, a brief description of the business models associated with successful on-going revenue generation and sustainability are included in this section. However, irrespective to the model chosen, there are relatively few RHIOs which have reached financial sustainability independent of major grant funding. Thus, fundraising is a vital component of a start-up RHIO business model.

There are at least three general business models that are being successfully implemented and generating revenue for RHIOs. These business models are utilizing at least two types of revenue sources. Each of these business models and each of the specific revenue sources will be discussed separately. Of particular note is that, at this writing, there is no example of a RHIO whose financial sustainability rests solely with either the sharing of clinical data or purely on a transaction-based fee structure.

Two of the RHIO business models presented (electronic commerce and service provision) are returning revenue and one innovative model (provider cost reduction) is still in the early stages.

Electronic Commerce

In the electronic commerce business model the RHIO is the preferred provider for the transmission of claims data between provider and payor. This model closely resembles other e-commerce models. Commonly a consortium of regional payors and providers, the emphasis is on the exchange of administrative data rather than clinical information. The advantage of this model is that near-term returns on investment are more easily seen when the costs per transaction can be substantially reduced to both providers and payors. Commonly cited examples include:
- UHIN—Utah Health Information Network
- NEHEN—New England Healthcare EDI Network

Providing a Service

In the service provision model the RHIO provides a variety of services to its members in addition or as a precursor to clinical data exchange. The service-based model defines specific service packages that are delivered to its members. The services may range from clinical messaging to EMR or electronic prescribing software access to EMR access capabilities. Commonly cited examples are:
- IHIE—Indiana Health Information Exchange

- HealthBridge—Greater Cincinnati area
- Kansas City area RHIO
- MHIN—Michiana Health Information Network

Clinical Messaging—Clinical messaging services can be implemented in a variety of ways. They can provide a common means for sharing data among organizations with formerly disparate and incompatible or expensive systems. A RHIO may become the common message carrier and replace the messaging systems of multiple providers with a common, less costly system. The providers pay the RHIO a usage fee which may be based upon a subscription or usage model.

Another messaging service to consider is where the RHIO becomes the outsourced solution for the delivery of results reporting for providers. In this instance laboratories and other providers outsource their content delivery to the RHIO.

Data Collection/Aggregation—RHIOs are particularly well positioned to be the point of data collection and aggregation for the tracking of public health surveillance. This is a service that can be provided to health departments and other health agencies for a fee. The collection and aggregation of chief complaint data from emergency departments is being undertaken by at least one RHIO and is producing a revenue stream.

Provide Access to Patient Demographic and Insurance Data—RHIOs will have access to demographic, as well as, clinical data and can be a provider of information to billing companies. There is at least one example, HealthBridge in Cincinnati, where a RHIO is providing billing companies with access to up-to-date patient information and are charging for the service of access to the data.

Medical Records Access—Access to medical records and other health-related data is seen as a key service that many RHIOs will provide. This service can be part of an overall quality improvement and cost containment package for which RHIOs can charge a fee. Administrative costs for reproduction are not uncommon and therefore this cost can more easily be integrated into existing budgets. A near-term ROI calculation could be based upon decreased paper and handling costs.

Provider Cost Reduction

There are many ideas regarding how RHIOs can be used to reduce the cost of care. Many of these models revolve around eliminating duplicate testing and unnecessary provider visits. While this model typically provides an obvious return to the payor, the ROI to the provider is less immediate and certainly less clear.

One model that directly reduces provider costs is based upon the notion of reducing costly and many times unnecessary and uncompensated emergency department (ED) visits by the uninsured or underinsured. This business model involves finding a "medical home" for these patients. Without a primary care physician patients many times use the ED for so-called "routine" visits or may hesitate to seek care when it is needed. Providing a primary care provider whom these patients can visit rather than making ED visits results both in fewer high cost, yet unnecessary visits to the ED and also the possibility of better continued care for the patients. The savings to the providers can be readily observed in a decrease in uncompensated episodes of care in the EDs.

A commonly cited example of this model is San Diego MINE—Medical Information Network Exchange.

Types of Revenue Sources

There are a variety of potential revenue sources that are possible, but two are currently generating revenue in RHIOs—membership/subscription fees and service-based fees. As RHIO models mature the results of some of the proposed future models will be able to be tested.

Membership and Subscription Fees—Many RHIOs combine membership and subscription fees in their revenue sources and these are usually associated with the e-commerce and cost reduction business models. In this type of model there is generally a basic membership fee assessed upon joining the RHIO. Subscription fees are then assessed on a monthly or annual basis. These fees may be set fees or fees based upon various classes of members. Examples of classes of members may include:

- Physician practices with sliding scale fees based upon practice size;
- Billing services whose fees are based upon the number of provider connections; and
- Hospitals with sliding scale fees based upon size.

Service-based Model—The service-based model sets charges for specific services delivered to customers. These services need to be well-defined and managed. Service level agreements (SLA) must be in place so that both the provider and recipient of services clearly understand what is being delivered and for what cost.

Service-based models often follow a subscription model where subscribers pay a set monthly fee which is determined by the service package being purchased. These packages may include, but are not limited to, messaging services, application service provider (ASP) models for electronic medical record software, Internet service provider access or shared infrastructure.

Other service-based models charge by the number of participants—for example, where major employers are participating in RHIOs for the purpose of access to clinical records for their insured employees—there are fees assessed per employee. In this instance the employees may opt out of the service if they desire.

Proposed Future Models

As stated previously, there are currently relatively few models so far shown to be financially sustainable. This does not mean, however, that other successful models may not emerge in the future. Much opportunity exists for the development and testing of additional potential models. The models listed below may have revenue-producing value but their value is not yet proven.

Public Health Informatics—RHIOs have the ability to provide high level data aggregation and reporting. This could be of great value to public health departments as part of an early warning and detection system for bio-events on a broad scale. Health departments could become subscribers to RHIOs for this service. Data can also be used for the identification and prediction of trends in public health.

Consumers—Data for Personal Health Records (PHR) will most likely be aggregated from a variety of provider sources. A subscription fee could be charged to the consumer from the RHIO for the aggregation, integration and transmission of this data.

Medical Device Manufacturers—The reluctance of physicians to adopt new device technology is a large barrier in the industry. RHIOs could facilitate "mini-trials" of new devices by providing large-scale evidence of proof of efficacy.

Pharmaceutical Companies—Already there is much discussion within pharmaceutical companies regarding how to take advantage of the sharing of medical information to facilitate clinical trials. Aggregate information could also be used to more quickly identify major adverse events associated with a specific drug or conversely provide on-going effectiveness of treatments. RHIOs could potentially contract with pharmaceutical companies to support their clinical trials research or post marketing follow-up.

Payor and Purchasers—This group is interested in data on the performance of physicians. A RHIO could aggregate performance data based upon a nationally recognized set of data and sell this to payors. This could take the form of aggregated performance data not specific to an individual payor.

Research—Academic informatics and research centers have many programs where clinical information is sought.

References

1. Agency for Healthcare Research and Quality (AHRQ) Evaluation Toolkit Web site.
2. eHealth Initiative. Second Annual Survey of State, Regional, and Community-Based Health Information Exchanges and Organizations.

CHAPTER 4

RHIOs and HIPAA

Steven J. Fox, David S. Szabo, and Howard A. Burde

RHIOs must maintain the privacy and security of protected health information (PHI) and must do so in a manner that complies with the Health Insurance Portability and Accountability Act (HIPAA) privacy and security standards. This is true despite the fact that these standards will not apply directly to most RHIOs, as most RHIOs will not be covered entities.[1] However, covered entities that participate in a RHIO by either providing data to the RHIO or obtaining data from the RHIO must comply with the privacy and security rules and will want to ensure compliance by the RHIO. Accordingly, RHIOs must build information privacy and security into both their technology and business processes. This chapter highlights some key privacy and security issues that will apply to most data exchange projects, and issues that are of particular relevance to developing RHIOs. It will address the applicability of HIPAA to the formation, organization and operation of RHIOs. This chapter is not intended to provide a comprehensive or in-depth discussion or analysis of the information privacy and security rule.

---

[1] HIPAA defines "covered entities" as (i) a health plan; (ii) (2) a healthcare clearinghouse; or (iii) a healthcare provider who transmits any health information in electronic form in connection with standard transactions. A RHIO that serves a clearinghouse function by translating non-standard transactions into standard format transactions, as defined by the administrative simplification rule, will be a covered entity subject to the information security and privacy rules in its own right. A clearinghouse can also be a business associate of a covered entity, however.

Privacy

Background: HIPAA Analysis

The general rule is that covered entities may only use or disclose PHI for treatment, payment or healthcare operations. Likewise, covered entities must protect the confidentiality, integrity and availability of electronic protected health information (ePHI) that they store, maintain, transmit or receive. By definition, RHIOs are involved in transmitting and receiving ePHI between and among covered entities, and some RHIOs, depending on their structure, may also store at least some elements of ePHI. For example, a RHIO that operates a master patient index or record locator service probably will store demographic data about patients, which is a subset of ePHI. Also dependent upon the architecture of the RHIO is whether or not it will act as a business associate of covered entities, and will have to comply with business associate privacy and security requirements, as well. If the RHIO is carrying out its activities "on behalf of" one or more covered entities, and requires access to PHI in order to carry out its activities, then the RHIO may well be a business associate, as defined by the HIPAA administrative simplification regulations, and must enter into a business associate agreement with the covered entity or entities. In the authors' experience, most RHIOs will be business associates.

However, not all organizations that move ePHI from one covered entity to another are business associates. Organizations that act only as passive "conduits" or switches for ePHI in transit are not considered business associates under HIPAA. Examples of these organizations include the post office and overnight parcel services (for physical movement of electronic media) and Internet service providers such as Utah Health Information Network. Even a specialized switch that moves ePHI in the form of encrypted messages might not be a business associate if it does not need access to PHI in order to perform its work.

In theory, a RHIO could subcontract all of its data exchange activities to a vendor or consultant, such that the RHIO itself never had access to ePHI. In that case, the RHIO entity itself would not be a business associate of the covered entities, but its prime vendor probably would be.[2] Every RHIO or data interchange organization should determine whether it is a business associate to covered entities. The covered entities will insist upon this when entering into business associate agreements with the RHIO.

Another less commonly seen RHIO structure is that of an organized healthcare arrangement (OHCA), where a group of covered entities holds itself out to the public as a joint arrangement, and participate in joint activities including utilization review, quality assessment and improvement activities, or payment activities involving financial risk sharing. At least two benefits of organizing a RHIO as an OHCA come readily to mind: (1) in addition to other permitted uses and disclosures of PHI, a participating covered entity may also disclose PHI about an individual to another participating covered entity for any healthcare operations activities of the OHCA; and (2) participating covered entities may satisfy the requirements for a notice of privacy practices (NPP) by a single

---

[2] A RHIO that creates standard processes for data interchange and provides technical services to its members through a common consultant or vendor could operate in this manner.

joint notice rather than multiple notices furnished by each individual covered entity, provided that certain additional requirements are met.[3]

If an OHCA structure is not used, each participating covered entity must separately provide an NPP to its patients. However, since each entity presumably has a different version of the NPP, it is essential that all NPPs are coordinated with common language and descriptions of the RHIO and the joint activities, risks/benefits for patients, and uses and disclosures that will flow from participation in the RHIO. The NPP may also be the appropriate vehicle with which to offer patients the opportunity to opt in or opt out of the RHIO. Some RHIOs are using a reverse opt-in mechanism, whereby patients are notified that if they do not affirmatively opt out, they will be automatically assumed to agree that their PHI may be included in the RHIO. This mechanism should be carefully reviewed and considered, because it has not been approved as yet by any regulatory or court decisions.

Uses and Disclosures of PHI

Whatever structure is ultimately decided upon for the RHIO, it may use or disclose PHI as follows:

- It may use or disclose PHI for the treatment, payment, or healthcare operations of a covered entity;
- It may disclose PHI for the treatment activities of a healthcare provider;
- It may disclose PHI to a covered entity or a healthcare provider for the payment activities of the recipient;
- It may disclose PHI to a covered entity for healthcare operations activities of the recipient, if each entity either has or had a relationship with the individual who is the subject of the PHI being requested, the PHI pertains to such relationship, and the disclosure is:
  — For a purpose listed in paragraph (1) or (2) of the definition of healthcare operations; or
  — For the purpose of healthcare fraud and abuse detection or compliance.

---

[3] (1) The participating covered entities agree to abide by the terms of the NPP with respect to PHI created or received by the covered entity as part of its participation in the OHCA;

(2) The joint notice meets the implementation specifications in paragraph (b) of § 164.520, except that the required statements may be altered to reflect the fact that the NPP covers more than one covered entity; and

    (i) Describes with reasonable specificity the covered entities to which the joint NPP applies;

    (ii) Describes with reasonable specificity the service delivery sites, or classes of service delivery sites, to which the joint NPP applies; and

    (iii) If applicable, states that the covered entities participating in the OHCA will share PHI with each other, as necessary to carry out treatment, payment or health care operations relating to the OHCA.

(3) The covered entities included in the joint NPP must provide the notice to individuals in accordance with the applicable implementation specifications of paragraph (c) of § 164.520. Provision of the joint NPP to an individual by any one of the covered entities included in the joint notice will satisfy the provision requirement of paragraph (c) of § 164.520 with respect to all others covered by the joint notice.

In addition to the general rules stated above, a RHIO must develop and implement comprehensive policies and procedures governing:

- Appropriate levels of role-based access to PHI for all participants and their employees;
- Comprehensive tracking and audit controls;
- Individuals' rights to agree or to object to specific uses/disclosures under certain conditions;
- Uses/disclosures for which an authorization or opportunity to agree or object is not required;
- Individuals' rights to request privacy protection and/or alternative communication methods for PHI;
- Individuals' rights of access to their PHI;
- Individuals' rights to amend their PHI;
- RHIO's accounting of disclosures of PHI; and
- Mechanism for participants to coordinate special patient arrangements with the RHIO.

One of the thorniest issues surrounding the use and disclosure of PHI is whether or not a patient authorization is required.[4] As discussed above, most uses/disclosures are permitted without asking a patient to sign an authorization, which is considered an extraordinary step under HIPAA. However, because of uncertainty in this area, some RHIOs are using authorizations as part of their standard operating procedure. Others, as previously mentioned, are simply using the NPP as a mechanism for presuming their patients' consent or approval for participation in the RHIO. There is no single answer that will work in all situations; however, the authors suggest a cautious approach for this matter. If it is decided to ask each patient for an authorization, remember that: (1) a covered entity may not generally condition the provision of treatment, payment, enrollment in a health plan or eligibility for benefits on the signing of an authorization by the patient; (2) all authorizations under HIPAA must contain an expiration date; (3) patients must be advised of their right to revoke the authorization at any time; and (4) the authorization must be written in plain language. So the use of authorizations will require a significant amount of additional bookkeeping, legal, and clerical time in order to assure compliance with the detailed regulatory provisions.[5]

There is another important consideration that must be dealt with regarding uses and disclosures of PHI, and that is the "minimum necessary" rule.[6] The general rule is that when using or disclosing PHI or when requesting PHI from another covered entity, a covered entity must make reasonable efforts to limit PHI to the minimum necessary to accomplish the intended purpose of the use, disclosure or request. Luckily, the rule does not apply to:

- Disclosures to or requests by a healthcare provider for treatment;
- Uses or disclosures made to the individual;
- Uses or disclosures made pursuant to an authorization under § 164.508;

---

[4] Keep in mind that § 164.508 requires an authorization for most uses and disclosures of psychotherapy notes.

[5] See § 164.508 for a detailed discussion of requirements for authorizations.

[6] See § 164.502(b).

- Disclosures made to the Secretary of the U.S. Department of Health and Human Services (HHS) in accordance with subpart C of part 160;
- Uses or disclosures that are required by law, as described by § 164.512(a); and
- Uses or disclosures that are required for HIPAA compliance.

Uses and disclosures for research purposes are beyond the scope of this guide, and add an additional level of complexity. If such use is contemplated, it may require approval by an Institutional Review Board or privacy board, and may also necessitate specific authorizations by affected patients as well as compliance with other federal and state laws and regulations.

Finally, although it is not necessarily required by HIPAA for non-covered entities, it may be advisable to appoint a RHIO-level privacy officer to interact with the various participants' own privacy officers and to ensure compliance with all of the rules, regulations and laws that will impact the operation and management of the RHIO. The privacy officer may also coordinate training among all of the RHIO participants, and oversee the adoption and use of the comprehensive policies and procedures (including sanctions) that will keep the RHIO functioning smoothly.

Security

This section will address organizational issues, risk assessment, safeguard selection, federated versus central security, and selected elements of the security management process.

Administrative Safeguards: Assigned Responsibility

A RHIO should formally assign responsibility for information security. While there is no formal requirement in HIPAA for a business associate to appoint a security officer, formal designation of this responsibility is likely to become a practical necessity. A RHIO can either designate one individual to act as its information security officer; or it can form a working group of security officers from sponsoring organizations. The creation of a working group is more likely to be the initial option, with a dedicated security officer coming later as the RHIO develops. Even after the appointment of a security officer, a security working group may be useful when implementing safeguards and monitoring their effectiveness.

A working group composed of several security officers has the advantage of providing multiple points of view to the security management process. Additionally, if the RHIO includes more than one type of covered entity or data source, then security expertise can be drawn from each type of organization. Since data sources often have different perspectives on risk that data users (usually being more risk averse), this diversity of viewpoints and perspectives can be extremely valuable to the planning process.

Administrative Safeguards: Risk Assessment

Covered entities must perform an assessment of the risks and vulnerabilities to the security of electronic protected health information, including an assessment of the likelihood and criticality of each security threat. Similarly, a RHIO also should formally assess risks arising from data exchange projects. Once the risks have been identified, the covered entities participating in the RHIO must be able to assure themselves that they or others have "implemented security measures sufficient to reduce risks and vulnerabilities to a reasonable and appropriate level."[7]

The RHIO should assess both the likelihood and criticality of threats to the security of ePHI. Events that are extremely unlikely or that, if they occur, are not of critical significance, are a lower priority than more probable threats or unlikely events that would have extremely serious consequences.

The security analysis should take into account the types of information being exchanged and maintained. For example, if information about mental health, substance abuse or HIV/AIDS is being exchanged, a higher level of confidentiality assurance and additional business process steps may be required.[8] Indeed, depending on the information and the state in which the RHIO operates, it might be necessary to filter certain information out of the data stream.[9] The RHIO should analyze the contemplated uses and disclosures of ePHI or "use cases" under both federal and state privacy laws, especially as state privacy laws often impose additional restrictions on certain types of data or types of covered entities.

The security analysis should take into account the technology employed for patient identification and data exchange. Messaging systems that only operate when a user affirmatively elects to send a message require different safeguards than "always on" connections through portals that can be accessed by data users without human intervention at the data source.

The security analysis should consider the number and types of personnel with access to ePHI. The number of users participating in the project might dictate the need for automated tools for authorizing users, issuing and revoking credentials and auditing user activities. In addition, the number of authorized users involved is a risk factor in and of itself, which the RHIO should account for in its planning process.

Once this analysis is complete, and any conditions on the use or disclosure of PHI are identified, security safeguards should be implemented to support the permitted uses and disclosures and prevent forbidden uses and disclosures. The RHIO should prepare written risk analysis and use it as a guide in the selection and implementation of the administrative, physical and technical safeguards that are being employed to protect the confidentiality, integrity, and availability of ePHI.

Selection and Implementation of Safeguards
The selection and implementation of safeguards is a key element of security compliance. The selection process should take into account whether particular safeguards are required by the security rule, or are only "addressable." Where a safeguard is "addressable" under the rule, the RHIO or its covered entities should adopt the safeguard if it is reasonable and appropriate under the circumstances. If the RHIO or covered entity chooses not

[7] This is the literal language of the rule; see 45 C.F.R. § 164.308(a)(1)(B).

[8] The security rule does not recognize any one type of PHI as deserving more protection than any other. Professional standards of practice as well as variations in state privacy and liability laws suggest otherwise.

[9] Filtering was used in the MEDSINFO ED Proof of Concept Project. See Gottlieb LK, Stone EM, Stone D, Dunbrack LA, Calladine J. PERSPECTIVE: Regulatory and Policy Barriers to Effective Clinical Data Exchange: Lessons Learned from MedsInfo-ED. Health Affairs. 24(5): Sept/Oct, 2005; 1197-1204.

to implement a safeguard, it must document why it would not be reasonable and appropriate, and implement "an equivalent alternative" measure, if reasonable and appropriate.

It may very well be that certain addressable safeguards, such as encryption for data being transmitted, are essentially required, in that no alternative safeguard will reasonably and appropriately protect the security of the information. Ideally, the RHIO's risk analysis, selection and implementation of safeguards will be clearly documented.

Some safeguards might be implemented through a federated model—that is, each covered entity will have delegated responsibility for implementing the safeguard within its organization on behalf of the RHIO. This is particularly appropriate where the RHIO does not handle data itself, but uses standards and contracts to facilitate peer-to-peer connections among the participating organizations.[10] Other safeguards, such as an activity monitoring system, might be implemented on a centralized basis by the RHIO itself.[11] The choice between federated and central security measures will require an analysis of the information architecture, security requirements, and the capabilities of participating covered entities.

The principle of "defense in depth" may lead to the implementation of both central and federated security measures. For example, an RHIO might have centrally maintained activity logs tracking all use of a data exchange application, while each covered entity will maintain its own logs documenting its uses of RHIO resources. Investigation of a privacy breach or security incident might require the use of both central and federated activity logs.

Every data exchange project needs to consider how to manage identities and access. Will the RHIO centrally issue credentials to users, or will it allow the participating covered entities to issue credentials? What legal obligations will remain with the users, and which ones will reside at the RHIO?

The RHIO should consider roles as an element of access control. A RHIO might implement role-based access controls and then require participating covered entities to adopt common administrative safeguards and delegate the authorization of users to each covered entity in accordance with common administrative rules or definitions.

The creation and assignment of roles requires an understanding of the business processes that will occur at the organizations using the data exchange system. For example, the RHIO must determine whether physicians will query the system directly, or will the physicians rely on nurses or administrative personnel to gather information at the point of care. The answer may vary from organization to organization, or even between departments in the same organization.

The practical ability of the RHIO to dictate the adoption of roles or other safeguards might depend on the criticality of the application or the degree to which the RHIO's proposed safeguards are consistent with safeguards that are already commonly accepted among the user community.

---

[10] This is the model for the New England Healthcare EDI Network, which facilitates administrative transactions among its participants.

[11] MA-SHARE implemented a central activity log as part of the portal for the MEDSINFO ED project.

The RHIO should have guidelines for the auditing of activity logs, including both automated reviews of system activities, and random manual audits for security purposes.

The risk analysis and legal requirements may require the implementation of special safeguards for certain types of data. Especially sensitive information, such as HIV/AIDS, mental health or substance abuse information, may require this kind of protection. For example, this information might need to be stored in locked records that cannot be shared among providers or released to other users without human intervention.

Security Management

The RHIO should develop a security management process that allows each covered entity to comply with the rule while participating in the RHIO. This would include developing a process for security collaboration among participating organizations. If a working group of security officers has been formed, this group might continue to meet in order to compare notes on possible security threats to the RHIO, review of activity reports, or to discuss real or alleged incidents involving the data exchange systems.

Collaboration among security officers will probably require them to focus on an agreed-upon definition of security incident. The group probably will want to prioritize their limited time to deal with significant threats to the system, not just review reports that have little or no security significance.

It is almost inevitable that some security incident or privacy breach will occur as a result of human error, a technical failure, or a novel attack. It is extremely important that the RHIO has agreed upon procedures for incident response, reporting and remediation. Because the RHIO is likely to be a business associate to several covered entities, once an incident is identified, the role of reporting and remediation probably will fall to the covered entities and not the RHIO itself.

There are several good reasons for RHIOs to play a support role, but not a primary role, when incidents occur. Unless the RHIO itself is a covered entity (which could occur if the RHIO is a clearinghouse), the primary obligation of security and privacy compliance falls upon the covered entities, which understandably will want to control any process of reporting and remediation of a breach or incident. Additionally, the investigation of a breach or incident may involve additional uses or disclosures of protected health information, much of which may not even be in the possession of the RHIO. Thus, the RHIO will probably limit its role to supporting or assisting the covered entities.

RHIO Agreements

Legal obligations relating to privacy and security must be taken into account in developing vendor and business associate agreements. RHIOs that outsource a significant portion of their data exchange activities should give considerable thought and attention to the requirements that they impose on key vendors and business associate subcontractors.

Many data exchange agreements and subcontracts simply state that each party will implement "reasonable and appropriate" safeguards. This language, drawn directly from the security rule, may be legally sufficient. However, the RHIO and its sponsors should consider carefully whether particular safeguards should be established as absolute minimum requirements for vendors.

Often, the discussion of safeguards begins and ends with technical safeguards, and a statement that "we can't dictate someone else's' technology." However, not all safeguards are technical, and even the adoption of common technical safeguards defined by categories does not mandate the use of particular vendors or technologies. For example, an administrative safeguard might include a requirement that all employees handling PHI be screened against exclusion and sanction databases maintained by the Office of Inspector General (OIG), or that criminal background checks be performed.

All business associate agreements require the reporting of privacy breaches and security incidents. However, the template agreement recommended by HHS does not mandate specific time frames for incident reports or particular content for incident reports.

Given the potential public relations and regulatory implications of a privacy breach or security incident, covered entities would be wise to ask for a very short time frame for an initial report (perhaps as short as one business day) with a longer time frame for a written follow-up report that includes a root cause analysis and discussion of remedial steps that have been or should be taken.

Vendors that play a key role in the RHIO, such as outsourcing or hosting companies, could be expected to sign agreements that are quite detailed with respect to information security. Other vendors may simply need to covenant to comply with the security rule. In every case, the criticality of the vendor's contribution to the project and the risks to security of ePHI should be considered in order to strike an appropriate balance.

RHIOs will enter into agreements with the covered entities that engage in data exchange projects, sometimes called participant agreements, end user agreements or data user agreements. Obviously, these agreements must define the services and technology to be provided by the RHIO, economic terms and other factors, but also should set forth both parties' mutual obligations with respect to privacy and information security. Indeed, the terms of these agreements are an essential part of the chain of trust that stretches from the RHIO's data sources to the data users. These agreements should set forth both the expectations of participants as data users and data sources, as well as the obligation that the RHIO must impose on the participants as part of the chain of trust.

One of the most difficult issues to think about or negotiate in data exchange agreements is indemnification from liability. An indemnification clause is a legal obligation to defend the other party to the contract from a claim asserted by a third person, and to pay any resulting settlement. For example, a provider of drug history data might say, "I will provide you with drug history data, but you have to defend me if a patient later sues me because you failed to protect the data, and the patient was injured as a result." Many risks, such as medical liability, patent infringement and others, potentially can be the subject of indemnification. While indemnification may be fair and reasonable in some circumstances, indemnification requirements can have a chilling effect on the willingness of organizations to participate in a data exchange project.

State Law Issues

In addition to HIPAA, each state has numerous laws which apply to the privacy of healthcare information. Each of these laws is a consideration in developing the rules of the network. The analysis begins with a determination of which of the state laws apply under HIPAA.

HIPAA regulations preempt "contrary" provisions of state law, with limited exceptions.[12] A determination of what is contrary is the first step in the HIPAA preemption analysis. Under the HIPAA regulations, a state law is contrary if a covered entity would find it impossible to comply with both the state law and with HIPAA or if complying with the state law would be an obstacle to fulfilling the requirements of HIPAA.[13]

Even when a state law is contrary to HIPAA, it would not be preempted when (1) the state law is necessary to prevent fraud and abuse, to regulate insurance or health plans, to regulate healthcare delivery, or to regulate controlled substances; (2) the state law relates to the privacy of health information and is more stringent than the HIPAA privacy rule; (3) the state law mandates public health reporting, investigation or intervention; or (4) the state law requires health plan reporting.[14]

The "more stringent than" rule is known as floor preemption. State laws with privacy provisions "more stringent than" HIPAA regulations are not preempted.[15]

State Health Information Privacy Laws

State laws regarding health information address a multitude of issues of interest to RHIOs: (1) To whom do such laws apply? (2) Under what circumstances may the information be transmitted? (3) What information may be transmitted? (4) What conditions apply to transmission of healthcare information?

Because many state laws which apply to PHI are or were written to regulate the practice of professions or the operation of facilities or health plans, they do not address PHI in the same manner as HIPAA, which is focused on the use of information. This is in part because most laws regulating healthcare preceded the HIPAA privacy and security regulations. It should be noted that several states have enacted laws which regulate health information in the insurance context.[16] These laws often address issues of consent and authorization, notice, amendment and other use questions. Other state laws, such as facility and health professional licensure regulations, tend to address the issues of content, ownership and storage of records. Still other laws, such as mental health and sexually transmitted disease laws, provide specific guidance with respect to spousal and parental access to information.

Indeed, most state laws will have no direct application to RHIOs, but because of the direct application to the regulated member of the RHIO, they must be considered. Other laws may not even apply to members of RHIOs, but nevertheless exist as part

---

[12] 42 C.F.R. Sec. 160.202.

[13] 42 C.F.R. Sec. 160.202.

[14] 42 C.F.R. Sec. 203.

[15] 45 C.F.R. § 160.203(b).

[16] See e.g., 28 Tex. Admin. Code § 22.52.

of the environment in which the RHIO is being created. For example, virtually every state's hospital licensure laws have medical record retention requirements.[17] By contrast, state laws which regulate the transmission of information regarding sexual assault may only apply to law enforcement or rape counselors, neither of which are likely to be considered covered entities or candidates for RHIO participation.

So, in creating an inventory of applicable laws, a RHIO should first determine what laws apply to the exchange of healthcare information. The next step will be to determine which laws actually apply to the activities in which the RHIO is engaged, or those activities in which the RHIO's members will be engaged. The RHIO and its members cannot be in the position of putting other members at risk of violating their licensure or other regulatory requirements.

The next level of analysis is determining what aspects or types of information may be transmitted and under what conditions. Laws that apply include, by way of example, insurance laws, genetic testing laws and disease specific laws. These laws must be compared to HIPAA privacy regulations for both contrariness and stringency to determine whether HIPAA or the state law will be applied to the transmission of health information through the RHIO. For example, a number of states have laws prohibiting medical laboratories from sending lab results to anyone other than the healthcare provider who ordered the tests. These laws could inadvertently have the effect of preventing the results from being timely sent directly to the RHIO; instead introducing an extra, unnecessary step in the process.

Disease-specific laws in each state provide guidance with respect to what HIPAA calls the minimum necessary rule. In practice this means the disease specific law often defines the scope of information that may be transmitted by a provider or otherwise identified person or entity. Common examples include HIV/AIDS, mental health, and substance abuse laws.

Laws pertaining to HIV/AIDS permit diagnostic test results to be released only to the patient and then, often, only with counseling. Further transmission of patient testing information is limited to the consent of the patient or, in the absence of such consent to notify those potentially infected by the patient.[18] Pennsylvania law permits disclosure to twelve designated categories of persons and entities for a circumscribed set of situations. For example, one designated category and situation is the provision which states that HIV/AIDS information may be released "if it would be necessary in case of emergency."[19] Not just any emergency, but only those when it would be "necessary." Given that this law also provides for a private right of action for breach of the privacy rights, this sort of silly locution is a potential trap for providers. To date it has not been the source of reported decisions against those who release information for the purposes of treatment. Nevertheless, it is this sort of problematic language that will impact RHIOs in one of three ways: (1) RHIOs will proscribe the transmission of such information absent explicit consent; (2) participants will transmit such information inconsistently; or (3) the RHIO and its participants will devote extraordinary time and

---

[17] See, e.g., 28 Pa. Code § 115.23.

[18] Texas Health Code Ann. § 81.101(5).

[19] 35 P.S. § 7607(a)(6).

resources to working through rules that apply to such information. The same sort of problematic laws exist in other disease specific laws as well.

Mental health laws contain restrictions on the transmission of different types of information. Most significantly, these restrictions often include limitations on the types of psychotherapy notes that may be transmitted as part of a claim for coverage.[20] For RHIO purposes, the question is what information a mental health provider may include as part of a record transmitted through the RHIO and for what purposes. Also, is the technology mature enough for such providers to distinguish electronically? In the absence of recognized limitations, will such providers participate? Extremely important in this discussion is whether the drug prescription information is included in the information shared through the RHIO as this information can indicate a mental health diagnosis indirectly.

Drug and alcohol treatment laws have the most stringent confidentiality provisions of any laws, virtually across all states. First, federal law provides that the "[r]ecords of the identity, diagnosis, prognosis or treatment of any patient" in a drug or alcohol program funded in whole or in part by the federal government (which means most of them) are confidential and may be released only if the patient has consented in advance to the disclosure or in the absence of disclosure (1) in the event of medical emergency; (2) for research, management audits, financial audits, or program evaluation; or (3) as mandated by court order.[21]

State laws tend to expand upon the federal confidentiality requirements. For example, the Pennsylvania Drug and Alcohol Abuse Control Act provides that patient records so obtained or patient records "relating to drug or alcohol abuse or drug or alcohol dependence prepared or obtained by a private practitioner, hospital, clinic drug rehabilitation or drug treatment center shall remain confidential and may be disclosed only with the patient's consent and only (i) to medical personnel exclusively for diagnosis and treatment; . . . or (ii) to government or other government officials exclusively for the purpose of obtaining benefits due the patient…[except for emergency situations for which records may be released] to proper medical authorities . . ."[22] Note the use of the conjunction "and" which means that even with the patient's consent drug and alcohol records may not be released beyond those two recipients. At least for RHIO purposes, the drug and alcohol rules are clear. Therein lies a fundamental conflict: the clarity of health information related laws is often inversely related to the need to transmit information. A strict prohibition is an easy rule to follow but inhibits the transmission of health care information which, after all, is the purpose of the RHIO.

What set or subset of medical records or other form of PHI may be exchanged? Each of the disease and covered entity specific state laws in some fashion define the scope of information covered.

Title XIX of the Social Security Act and state laws which pertain to Medicaid programs also address the privacy of healthcare information. Federal law requires state medical assistance plans to "provide safeguards which restrict the use or disclosure

---

[20] 740 ILCS 110/6.

[21] 42 U.S.C. § 290dd-2; see also 42 C.F.R. part 2.

[22] 71 P.S. § 1690.108(c); see also 4 Pa. Code § 255.5.

[23] 42 U.S.C. 1396a(a)(7).

of information concerning applicants and recipients to purposes directly connected with administration of the plan."[23] Federal Medicaid regulations implementing this requirement define "purposes directly related to plan administration" to include providing services for recipients.[24]

Under most state laws and Medicaid managed care organization contracts, identifiable health information may be shared with a provider where such information is required for treatment purposes without patient consent, so long as the recipient will treat the information confidentially and not use it for other purposes.[25] Medicaid law, therefore, does not inhibit health information exchange.

Liability and Indemnification

RHIOs and their participants face two types of liability related to the use of health information: breach of privacy obligations and professional/medical malpractice liability.

Breach of privacy obligations may arise from case law or from specific statutory recognition of the cause of action. While the HIPAA enforcement mechanism is oversight by HHS and the U.S. Justice Department, many state laws specifically provide for private enforcement action. One of the more profound impediments to RHIO formation is the negotiation regarding the delegation of responsibility for the transmission of healthcare information inappropriately, and for the content of the information provided. As RHIOs are relatively new entities and the law on the topic of healthcare information privacy is not well developed, so the availability and cost of insurance coverage specific to such risk is uncertain. Presumably, the RHIO will require that its members maintain some sort of umbrella liability policy governing general errors and omissions which might be specifically written to include inadvertent release of healthcare information. Such a rule, of course, presumes that an insurer will be willing to underwrite the risk of inadvertent or inappropriate release of health information.

By contrast, the law of medical malpractice liability is very well developed. The question raised by the use of healthcare information transmitted in a health information exchange is who bears the liability for the content of the information exchanged, whether the consolidation of information into a common form creates medical malpractice or another form of liability (which impacts the use of experts and potentially, depending upon the state, the amount of recovery), and whether the existence of an available source of information specific to a patient creates an obligation on the part of the provider to consult that source of information.

By way of short background, the elements of any medical malpractice case are few: There must be an injury or adverse event; the standard of care, established by expert testimony, must have been breached; and the breach must be the proximate cause of the injury.

Therefore, placing health information exchange in the medical malpractice context, the question is how the standard of care will be interpreted and applied. Will the standard of care ultimately include responsibility on the part of each participant

---

[24] 42 C.F.R. § 431.302.

[25] See 55 Pa. Code § 105.3.

in a health information exchange to validate the information transmitted through the RHIO? Will the standard establish the responsibility of a treating provider to obtain available sources of information? Will the standard establish the responsibility of parties, such as payor to provide information to the health information exchange?

The standard of care with respect to healthcare provider use of available information is evolving. To the extent that the entire development of American liability law recognizes that adoption of innovations leads to developments of higher expectations and therefore higher standards of care, we can expect that the increased availability of healthcare information in an inexpensive and useful format will lead to a standard of care which establishes the responsibility of the provider to use such information. Innovation leads to higher standards, witness fetal monitoring and glaucoma cases (see e.g., *Helling v. Carey*).[26]

RHIOs and their participants need also be concerned that the developing standards include responsibilities for the accuracy of information in the exchange. To that end, who determines accuracy of content of health information? Who is responsible for correcting PHI? Whose version of events/diagnoses prevails? What is the impact of practice enhancements on health professional liability or on the payors that pay for performance?

To the extent that the RHIO engages in these activities, it is creating a source of liability which cannot be avoided. Ultimately, such issues will not be resolved by the RHIO or its participants, but rather the responsibility for the potential liability will be negotiated as part of the participation agreement among the participants. That negotiation will result in an agreement to the parameters for responsibility for breaches of the standard of care, indemnification for actions which may implicate the RHIO and the other participants, and insurance coverage for potential losses. While it would be helpful to have a common tool to assess potential risk to each party in exchange, including the exchange or RHIO, such a tool may be too difficult to establish. It is likely to be much easier, though more expensive, for the parties to agree to bear and insure risk for own actions. This agreement would be supplemented by common insurance for collective risks as a means to allay concerns.

---

[26] Supreme Court case: Helling v. Carey 83 Wash. 2d 514, 519 P.2d 981 (1974).

CHAPTER 5

Patient Identification and Matching

Lorraine Fernandes, RHIA, and Jim Younkin

Health information exchange is expected to produce many positive results, including increased patient safety, reduced duplicate testing, increased regulatory compliance, and higher patient satisfaction. With high user expectations regarding patient identification, it is essential that RHIOs ensure that the right patient records can be located, on demand and in real time, across various disparate systems. This chapter discusses the challenges of matching, linking, and identifying patients to help inform the reader on how to choose technology for this critical task.

Accurate patient identification and matching begins at the local entity (source) level in the master person index (MPI). Unfortunately, the average error rate (one individual having multiple medical record numbers) in a local-entity level MPI is 8%–15% due to lack of data quality processes, immature technology in the 1980s and 1990s, and consolidation of MPIs as integrated delivery networks were formed without regard to "common" patients. Much of this resulted from first generation enterprise master person index (EMPI) software lacking technical sophistication and scalability, thereby creating a lack of appreciation for the importance of patient ID as the foundation to electronic medical records. In fact, the EMPIs created in the 1990s frequently contain error rates of 15%–30%. Third generation EMPI software can overcome these inherited challenges and allow RHIOs to deliver the quality, scalability, and speed that users expect.

Given the high expectations and anticipated results from health information exchange, coupled with a general belief that creating a national identifier will not happen in the U.S. in the near term, if ever, there have been considerable industry and consumer advocacy discussions about patient identification and matching. Many discussions reference the Canadian decision not to issue a national healthcare identifier and the provinces' use of EMPI software for patient identification. Additionally, while most European countries have a national healthcare identifier, they frequently augment patient identification with EMPI software.

Essentially, each health information exchange (HIE) requires enough distinguishing information about each patient to accurately identify a patient across various systems of the participating organizations. Many patients want to protect much of their personally identifiable information, especially in the wake of media stories about identity theft and fraud. Patients want to be assured that their information will be protected and not fall into the wrong hands. However, patients also want the benefits of information exchange, including more informed medical personnel. Patients would rather give their information once, upon initial admission to a healthcare system or a RHIO, than repeat the same information at each stage of the process, from the emergency department to the lab to the pharmacy, thus minimizing the risk of error. Hence, consumer involvement in HIE may take many routes, including the ability to monitor when information has been requested, when it was released, and to whom.

Protection and control by patients and consumers must be weighed against the need of information availability for a health information exchange to have value. Healthcare providers want a more complete profile for each patient within their own systems but are reluctant to share certain elements with other facilities. At the same time, much of the information collected falls under HIPAA regulations and may require special considerations to manage, share and protect this protected health information (PHI).

EMPI systems, which will generally be used by RHIOs, offer varying degrees of security, including the latest in encryption technology and firewall protection. When sharing this information with other facilities, security settings restrict who can see what information, obscuring more sensitive data while ensuring the sharing of pertinent medical information.

The uniqueness and frequency of data should have a major impact on matching capability, yet the HIE may set minimum data standards for participation. Encryption of data at various points in transmission and storage will be explored. Safeguarding particularly sensitive data elements that assist in probabilistic matching, particularly Social Security numbers (SSN) is very important and required for compliance with a growing number of state regulations and legislation. Therefore, RHIOs may choose to not capture SSN, capture but not display to a query, only use the last four digits of the SSN, or make other business decisions regarding this data element. Probabilistic matching can transcend these decisions by using whichever data elements are available and visible from each source system.

The Debate: Identifiers and Exact Match vs. Algorithmic Matching

Matching patients to their records is at the core of any health information exchange initiative, whether for integrated delivery networks (IDNs), RHIOs or other groups. Current processes are often tedious and do not necessarily produce accurate results without manual intervention. Patients are often responsible for recounting their own medical history when previous records are not available, cannot be found or are incomplete. This becomes especially problematic when patients are incapacitated and unable to describe their history or omit something crucial. The young, elderly, and chronically ill—those most in need of accurate medical history—are the most vulnerable to this problem.

As RHIOs form, they must tackle the issue of patient identification and accurate record linking. Connecting for Health, a public-private collaborative funded by the Markle Foundation and Robert Wood Johnson Foundation, strongly believes that accurately matching patient records enables the searching and sharing fundamental to interoperability and data exchange.[1] As a result, some RHIOs may be tempted to create their own RHIO-specific unique identifier, but this would require the use of EMPI technology. Therefore, one might ask, "why bother?" Others suggest using a single, unique identifier to track patients and their records across facilities or regions. Some groups advocate using the SSN, while others believe a new national identifier for healthcare should be established. However, there are important issues that arise with any unique identifier that should be carefully weighed before moving forward.

Some unique identifier advocates assume that assigning a new national healthcare identifier will solve the problem of accurately identifying the patient, as all records could be linked to this identifier. This assumption is incorrect, however, because any such identifier would need to be introduced into a world of existing data, and some means is needed to link data to the new identifier without the benefit of one. This circumstance in and of itself makes the case for probabilistic matching, where algorithms that account for discrepancies in data are used to more precisely match data from various sources. Deterministic matching, which relies on matching based on identical data elements across sources, was used years ago for small-scale patient matching. But it has been shown not to scale well to hundreds of thousands or millions of persons. As a result, many organizations and vendors have turned towards probabilistic matching because it has the power to manage systems with hundreds of millions of people where data anomalies are inevitable. This section articulates the pluses and minuses of each approach, and gives concrete suggestions for RHIOs addressing this issue.

This country's experience with Social Security numbers should serve as a cautionary tale for any new government-issued unique identifier. From its inception in the 1930s, the SSN was not to be used for identification purposes—this statement was even printed on the cards themselves. However, as agencies and private companies began to use the number as a *de facto* unique identifier, problems developed ranging from fraud and abuse to identity theft. As a result, many Americans are increasingly protective about their SSNs.

A new government identifier would likely face similar challenges to protect users from fraud and misuse. Additionally, a unique national identifier is only useful with universal adoption, something nearly impossible with immigrants and temporary workers and visitors who may need medical care but lack the nationally-distributed identifier.

From a technology standpoint, many legacy systems could not accommodate a new mandatory field (that would require checking digits if any acceptable level of accuracy was to be achieved) without incurring substantial costs. And adding a new unique identifier to already fragmented or incomplete records would only complicate the identification puzzle by potentially assigning numerous numbers to a single person or by not linking existing records to their owner. Rather than solving the problem, it creates new problems by creating another field that can be marred by inconsistent use or data entry errors.

Many privacy and security concerns arise when discussing a new national healthcare identifier as it would be subject to identity theft and mis-use, as is the case with SSNs today. Additionally, there are issues of the cost and effort of issuing, administering and promulgating a national identifier.

A voluntary national healthcare identifier (VNHID) and associated implementation guidelines have been proposed by the American Society for Testing and Materials (ASTM), with balloting underway. In general, the standard would support an "open" universal healthcare identifier (UHID) as well as 31 classes of encrypted healthcare identifiers (EUHIDs) that have varying levels of restrictions. An identifier, if not already assigned and stored by the applicable EMPI, would be requested from the national organization supporting the voluntary identifier standard, thus security is tightly controlled and totally electronic. While only one UHID would likely exist, many EUHIDs could exist. With a known UHID or EUHID, a distributed query could be launched to all other EMPIs to gather relevant, authorized information. This approach, which is heavily dependent on EMPIs, manages the risk of errors in patient matching, as well as privacy and confidentiality. Drawbacks include defining and funding startup, expenses, a sponsoring organization, and patient participation.[1]

As a result, more IT professionals and EMPI approaches began to rely on probabilistic matching, which uses a combination of readily available data, such as name, birth date, ZIP code and address to accurately identify and link patient records. While SSNs can be used in patient matching, either in whole or only the last four digits, it is not required. Since probabilistic matching can improve the rate and quality of matched records by considering more of a database's characteristics, it can better overcome discrepancies in data collection or data entry errors to provide accurate matches with fewer false positives and false negatives.

Probabilistic matching recognizes that simply assigning a new identifier does not guarantee consistent and accurate person identification. Rather, probabilistic matching can use the identifier as yet another matching attribute, if one such number is ever adopted in the U.S., but the successful patient matching is not reliant on the existence of this number. Probabilistic matching takes into account *all* of the attributes, that, when combined, lead to a high probability or likelihood of linking information. The more fields compared by probabilistic matching, the better the determination of accurate and false matches.[2] In addition, research recommends probabilistic matching for situations that require more sensitivity or accuracy—both essential to patient medical records.[1]

When the Canadian government began working with Canada Health Infoway to develop a nationwide electronic health information system, the new national identifier debate was short lived, and in fact deemed a non-starter. Rather, Canada adopted its client registry system based on probabilistic matching that is adaptable to each province's unique needs, but the system can accommodate a national identifier if Canada changed direction in the decades ahead. RHIOs can learn valuable lessons from such a system and adopt a probabilistic matching system that offers the best patient identification and matching to protect patient health and safety while still having the option in the decades ahead to add a national healthcare identifier if one is created.

How to Pick a Patient Identification and Patient Matching Tool

For RHIOs, a foundation of accurate patient identification is a fundamental requirement for success. By their nature, RHIOs require an accommodation for disparate data and systems, varied standards of data collection, mixed data quality, and incongruent collection mechanisms require technology solutions which will enable integration and interoperability without requiring participants to invest in new systems and processes to participate.

When looking for a patient identification tool, RHIOs need to evaluate some key criteria to ensure that the tool will meet initial goals, as well as future needs. Some of the most important considerations are discussed below.

Algorithms

Patient identification tools generally support three distinct types: deterministic matching, ad hoc scoring/matching, and probabilistic algorithms. A deterministic approach, which was dominant in legacy systems in the 1980s and 1990s, examines a subset of attributes and marks two records as referring to the same member if they agree on these attributes. Deterministic matching relied on exact matches of demographic information, either entire fields or a limited number of characters of the fields. A simple example would be to link two records if they agreed on last name, first name and phone number or a portion of the last name, first name and SSN, generally on a byte-for-byte comparison. The two main drawbacks to this approach are that it often overlooks matches because of variations in data values (e.g., "ROBERT" versus "BOB") and that this approach does not scale well to large datasets because it does not account for attribute frequency; that is, a match on the last name "SMITH" does not mean as much as a match on the last name "EINSTEIN."

This approach is not as accurate as other approaches and faces a large number of false negatives because it could be impaired by typographical errors, name changes, nicknames and other differences in demographic information. Additionally, the deterministic approach produces high volumes of false positives, as it does not address the commonality of names and other fields. The deterministic approach also struggled to scale as high volumes of records were added.

Ad hoc scoring/matching allows the determinations of how to score data elements that contribute to a match. Weights for the matching attributes are generally determined by the customers, with little or no guidance for mathematical relevance. Thus, scores are arbitrary and the general mathematical or human rationale of the higher the score the greater the probability that the match is accurate is not true. The drawback this produces for a RHIO, in particular, is in working with the stakeholders to determine the threshold for presuming a "solid" match.

Probabilistic matching, on the other hand, avoids the drawbacks of deterministic matching by recognizing the variability in attribute values and incorporating that knowledge into the matching decision. Further, the best algorithms are based upon mathematical principles that accommodate the frequency and uniqueness of data attributes. Probabilistic matching allows the greatest flexibility and provides the highest accuracy. Neither sharing identifiers (e.g., SSNs) nor using a deterministic matching method will accurately match records when faced with large variances in the data. A sound mathematical model should serve as the foundation for the algorithm, with updates based on research, experience and industry trends.

Even for those solutions that do support probabilistic patient record comparison, MPI vendors may use a standard weight table based on national or regional standards. The most accurate results are achieved when an algorithm uses a weight table based on the client's actual MPI and its specific characteristics. This will become very critical for RHIOs, as by definition they will support disparate but distinct populations.

Additionally, algorithms need to account for different naming conventions (including those within specific ethnic groups) used by each participating organization, equivalence names (i.e., nicknames), as well as phonetic matching. These functions will be minimal to ensure successful patient identification, and any quality algorithm should offer even broader functionality to account for address variation, additional identifiers (including those that may be proposed in the future) and varied phone numbers.

Finally, the patient identification tool should support configurability, to ensure that as the RHIO population changes and grows; the algorithm can be tuned to support the varied requirements.

RHIOs using probabilistic matching include CareSpark, MA Share and Indiana Health Information Exchange.

Accuracy and Scalability

The patient identification tool selected by a RHIO needs to provide accurate patient information that is based upon a sound statistical model. While this seems redundant, a large number of patient matching tools on the market do not use an algorithm that is sufficiently robust and accurate to support this fundamental requirement. If a RHIO does not first *accurately* represent the medical information for participants, it can not succeed. Patient safety and security require that all relevant and appropriate information about a patient be available to RHIO participants. Consumers will insist that information about them be precise and complete. RHIOs must invest in a quality product to help them achieve their vision of effective healthcare data exchange.

How RHIOs structure and define themselves varies from one geographic area to another. RHIOs do, however, have some things in common, including a requirement for growth. In fact, a RHIO might start its health information exchange with a single project that involves 100,000 records, do a second that encompasses 500,000 records and ultimately reach 5 million records or more at full deployment. This requires that any patient identification strategy be scalable, as "swapping out" technology would squander precious time, human and financial resources.

Scalability, in this case, really means two things: an ability to support larger populations and integrate more applications, as well as an ability to support new and changing data requirements and industry standards. This will require products to have robust application architecture and an open and configurable data model, requirements that cannot be underrated. Additionally, integrating with very disparate systems requires a product architecture that delivers the tools to enable this. As data needs evolve, it is critical that the data model is flexible enough to scale to meet new requirements.

Threshold Setting

Threshold setting establishes a standard for records to be "matched" and presented to a query, and also designates how to handle potential matches where human intervention and review may be employed. RHIOs may or may not require either of these thresholds to be established. Setting thresholds determines how patient identification will be managed; hence, it is critical that they are set carefully. Threshold setting is a significant business decision based on the algorithm in use and the user community's expectations.

Since RHIOs may want to support different standards for establishing matching record sets based on participation, user profiles, governance or other unique reasons, a quality patient identification tool should have configurable threshold. Additionally, RHIOs may need to adjust the established thresholds over time, as data quality improves or participation grows. Thresholds might be set unique to specific categories of users. For example, emergency department physicians might require a different threshold than a radiology department. Finally, the vendor who provides the patient identification tool should have expertise in being able to establish the optimal threshold (which will ensure the most accurate result sets)—and be willing to assist RHIOs as part of their implementation effort.

Data Presentation

Consumers of RHIO data will vary widely across the continuum of care, raising governance and security concerns that must be addressed when defining data presentation. The patient identification tool should support these concerns in at least two distinct ways:

- Offer robust role-based security and audit tracking. This will enable RHIO governance teams to minimally understand what data has been seen, when and by whom; and
- Offer robust configurability of the content of actual patient identities. In order to establish different 'views' of the patient, the patient identification tool must have functionality to enable this requirement.

For example, the SSN represents one data element that generates increasing controversy when captured, used in assisting patient matching and included as part of data presentation. A RHIO might decide to use all or part of the SSN in matching, and display only the last four characters in data presentation, thereby enhancing matching but not compromising patient privacy.

Patient identification tools cannot just establish and link the correct patient identification information; they must also represent the patient's record to consuming applications. This will require that the patient identification tools allow defined applications—and ultimately users—to determine how data should look, and who has access to that information. Various integration options, which include the configurability to define different data representations, will be critical to support of ongoing RHIO business and process requirements. These options should include robust APIs, including the latest data integration standards and technologies, like Java, Web Services and HL7 Query/Response, to name a few.

Establishing and Maintaining Data Quality

Based on system capability, resources, and RHIO-established requirements, data quality will vary across the RHIO-participant continuum, underlining the need for data quality standards. A patient identification tool needs to consume data of varying quality, while supporting accurate patient identification. Some RHIOs might actually establish minimum data standards for participation, or enact them over time. Thus the patient identification tool must be able to quantify and report the data quality that is reflected at the source system/RHIO partner level. The tool should also be configurable enough to include various data structures and content.

The patient identification product offering should include an application which provides mechanisms for maintaining data quality at multiple levels. Basic considerations include whether minimum content standards are being met, how "correctly" data has been collected, and (potentially) how to manage established patient identities. Additionally, this tool should also optionally allow for various RHIO participants to have access to their "own" data to improve their overall data quality. This will aid participants, as well as the RHIO, because better data ensures greater trust among RHIO participants, and will hopefully encourage expanded RHIO use.

Reporting Tools or Metrics

The patient identification tool should include some mechanisms for reporting on metrics for success, as established by the RHIO's leadership, and require access to data to evaluate how effectively the metrics will be met. Reporting tools may be available either within the EMPI software or through business intelligence tools to achieve this, and should also be configurable and flexible to accommodate changing needs. As RHIOs establish and update their goals and objectives, they will require a means to evaluate their success, so the technical environment should be able to manage a multitude of reporting requests.

Implementation Strategies and Timelines

The experience and expertise of the organization providing the selected product suite will drive some recommendations about implementation strategies and timelines. The implementation plan should account for RHIO goals, varied partner integration strategies, data quality considerations and algorithm configuration, among other things. Implementation timelines will vary based upon selected products and number of source systems, but as a rule of thumb, should span less than six months. Defining data elements for patient matching and threshold setting, as outlined above, will likely be key tasks in the implementation and have a major impact on user acceptance. The implementation plan will have to accommodate sites that have HL7 messaging and interface engines, sites that have no messaging infrastructure and therefore will have to submit in batch on a scheduled basis, and sites that will not be able to submit data, but will have users querying data for patient matching.

Flexibility and configurability of the patient identification tool will be key to the success of the overall RHIO implementation plan.

Impact of Centralized, Decentralized, and Hybrid Data Models to Patient Matching/Identification

By virtue of multiple organizations being involved in HIE, irrespective of which model of data storage is elected by the RHIO, it is fundamental that the patient first be identified before anything can be exchanged. Regardless of the model—central, federated or hybrid—there is consistent need for accurate patient matching. While one might think that a centralized repository escapes this fundamental challenge, even it will be rendered useless if patient information cannot be linked between the contributing data sources. This section explores each data model, and highlights the needs for accurate patient matching at various points in the information flow (see also Table 5-1). In most cases, an EMPI will be used to link patient identifiers from the contributing sources and organizations.

Table 5-1. Impact of Centralized, Decentralized, and Hybrid Data Models to Patient Matching/Identification

	Centralized Data Model	Decentralized/Federated Data Model	Hybrid Data Model
Unique features	Information is aggregated into a shared repository containing data from all sources	Allows the data to be physically stored behind their firewalls at the originating organizations, not stored remotely with data from other sources	A cross between a centralized and decentralized architecture, having elements of both
How it handles patient ID/ matching when storing information	Allows duplicative data or uses a matching scheme (e.g., EMPI) to find matches to associate with upon data insert	Generally an EMPI will house a limited amount of patient demographic information to facilitate patient identification and record location among sources, commonly referred to as a record locator service (RLS)	Varies as portions of data are aggregated centrally while some remains federated, requiring different handling when stored
How it handles patient ID/ matching when accessing information	Looks up data based on deterministic matching on an enterprise identifier	A request to the central index (EMPI) to access a patient's records results in a list of locations where a patient has records	Would likely mirror a federated model, whereby an EMPI with a probabilistic algorithm would be used
Unique issues	Deceptively appears to avoid patient matching challenges, but still faces them on data insert	PHI can readily be excluded from a federated model	A determination is made about what kind of clinical data should be centralized vs. federated with the same question asked about patient ID, and the technology and policy discussions are intermingled

All data models will have the common challenges of how to address record retrieval and patient ID in the context of data quality, opt-in, opt-out, and managing sensitive PHI such as HIV, mental health, and pregnancy.

Centralized Data Model

What Is Unique about This Model?
The centralized data model is one in which patient information is aggregated into a shared repository containing data from all sources. The repository may contain only clinical information and therefore be considered a clinical data repository (CDR), or it may contain additional demographic, administrative or insurance information in which the term "data warehouse" may be more appropriate.

How Is Patient ID/Matching Handled When Information Is Stored?
On the surface one may think that patient identification and patient matching are not an issue in the centralized model because the data is stored in a central repository. In fact, it is possible to accept all data in its native format and numbering scheme and store the information logically by facility. However, this puts a heavy burden on the retrieval process to determine which records belong to the same patient, and the risk of not establishing the appropriate patient identity is high. Therefore, it is likely that the process of populating the repository includes a function to first determine if the patient exists in the repository and then to link the new information with the existing with some kind of internal enterprise identifier that will be unknown to the outside world. The patient ID importance remains, even if a single vendor is also the vendor to the source systems and the repository, as each contributing source system will have their unique naming conventions, data capture methods, and potentially HL7 (Health Level Seven) messaging versions.

An EMPI will normally be used for the patient ID. When the repository interface engine receives patient information, it will call the EMPI using the patient demographics and local identifier (usually medical record number) to determine if the patient already has information in the repository. If so, the new record is tagged with the internal enterprise identifier and stored in the repository. If no matching records are found, then a new enterprise identifier is generated and the information is stored in the repository. When information about the same patient is later sent to the repository, this information will be stored with the new enterprise ID, even if it originated from another source organization. This model requires that the CDR support potential changes to the enterprise ID, as patient identification information may shift over time. This can be very difficult for CDRs to support, as they are not architected to manage enterprise level identifiers and data.

How Is Patient ID/Matching Handled When Information Is Accessed?
Information requested from a central repository is typically handled by a web server or interface engine through a query/response mechanism. A browser or client application requests information from the repository, and the Web server or interface engine serves up the information from the repository. The information may have been stored using

an enterprise identifier, so the server application must have enough information in the request in order to identify the patient in the EMPI. If the requestor has a local identifier, such as a medical record number from a local facility, it can be used to perform a deterministic patient match in the EMPI. If only demographic information is known, as would be most common in HIE, the probabilistic matching algorithm within the EMPI would be used to facilitate patient ID. The EMPI may be accessed through an API or other means such as Web services provided the CDR can support these mechanisms (often they cannot). Once the enterprise identifier is determined, it is used to retrieve the requested data for that patient.

What Unique Issues Exist?

The issues with this model are similar to others, with the exception that initially participants may think this methodology avoids the patient ID challenge, thus creating risk and additional work later in the technology and work process design. Additional challenges may exist particularly if sensitive clinical information related to diseases such as mental illness are included in the repository. If all clinical information is sent to the repository, extreme care must be taken to ensure that the patient ID and information exchange process are compliant with state and federal laws that may place restrictions on certain diagnoses or treatments. Thus workflow and processes must be defined to not answer the patient ID query, lest clinical data be erroneously released. Finally, this approach requires that CDRs be able to support particular architecture scenarios, which may be difficult depending on the kind of system and expected use. Careful and intertwined consideration is required when discussing identification and centralized data storage.

Decentralized/Federated Data Model

What Is Unique about This Model?

The decentralized, or federated, model of health information exchange gives greater control to the organizations that generate the data by allowing the data to be physically stored behind their firewalls. The data may be modified to a standard format for easy lookup by a central indexing system or may be retrieved via a "gateway" type of access. With a gateway approach, the query will not directly "hit" the clinical source system, but rather the gateway contains the subset of information that is available to external queries.

How Is Patient ID/Matching Handled When Information Is Stored?

With this approach for a RHIO, generally an EMPI will house a limited amount of patient demographic information to facilitate patient identification and record location, commonly referred to as a record locator service (RLS). The subset of patient demographic data necessary for patient ID and linking is generally captured at the launch, with HL7 or other standard messaging being utilized thereafter to keep the EMPI consistent with patient activity at the source level. The clinical data is stored locally in a standard format, using the local organization's identifier to access the record.

Additional details about RLS can be found in the Connecting for Health Common Framework documents of April 2006.

Alternatively, if an EMPI already exists "in front of" the federated clinical data, this schema could support peer-to-peer queries for patient identification. With this scenario, the limited subset of patient demographic data would not be required, as the patient ID process would be handled through API calls or other messaging that would be from EMPI to EMPI. This structure is anticipated in the Client Registry deployments (HIE) across the Canadian provinces.

How Is Patient ID/Matching Handled When Information Is Accessed?

A request to the central index (EMPI) to access a patient's records results in a list of locations where a patient has records. This request does not necessarily occur as part of the transaction management (as with the CDR version above), but rather at the point the HIE application requires it. This can reduce processing overhead, as well as increase accuracy.

What Unique Issues Exist?

PHI can readily be excluded from a federated model, allowing facilities as whole, or specific types of care centers to opt out.

Hybrid Data Model

What Is Unique about This Model?

A hybrid data model is a cross between a centralized and decentralized architecture. For example, the eHealth Volunteer Initiative in Tennessee uses a system where the data is physically stored and managed in a central location, but the data is logically separated into "vaults" controlled by each organization that contributes data.

How Is Patient ID/Matching Handled?

As with the centralized system, the need for patient identification does not change since data is being contributed from numerous sources with their own messaging, formats, and unique data capture features. These challenges exist, even if a single vendor is proving the repository, as each contributing source system will have their unique naming conventions, data capture methods, and potentially HL7 messaging versions. Operationally, this can be challenging, because a determination would have to be made about what kind of clinical data should be centralized versus federated with the same question asked about patient ID. Therefore, the technology and policy discussions are intermingled.

How Is Patient ID/Matching Handled When Information Is Stored?

The hybrid method would likely mirror a federated model, whereby an EMPI with a probabilistic algorithm would be used for patient identification and record location.

How Is Patient ID/Matching Handled When Information Is Accessed?
The specifics of the hybrid model will determine the information query structure. In some cases (like the CDR model), the patient identities may be managed at the time the transactions are processed; others (like the federated approach) may establish clinical data aggregation at the point of request.

References

1. Connecting for Health, Working Group for Accurately Linking Information for Health Care Quality and Safety. Linking Health Care Information: Proposed Methods for Improving Care and Protecting Privacy. February, 2005.
2. Gomatam S, Carter R, Ariet M, Mitchell G. An empirical comparison of record linkage procedures. *Statistics in Medicine.* 21 (2002):1485-96.

CHAPTER 6

RHIO Technology Case Studies

Peter T. van der Grinten and Charles W. Jarvis, FACHE

Current Status of RHIOs and Their Structure

HIMSS defines a RHIO as a multi-stakeholder organization that enables the secure exchange and use of patient health information among clinicians and caregivers to improve the delivery, efficiency, quality, and safety of patient care.

A Forrester Research report from March 2006 notes that while hundreds of RHIOs are in the talking stages, very few are operational. The majority of RHIOs are working on determining how best to structure the governance and oversight of their operations and whether to link their efforts with state-sponsored health information exchange (HIE) initiatives. A July 2006 report from eHealth Initiative[1] notes that nearly 30 states are undertaking efforts to speed the development of health information networks, including RHIOs, as a way to improve the quality and cost effectiveness of patient care.

Through its online site HIT Dashboard,[2] HIMSS lists more than 50 functional RHIOs across the U.S., and also shares details on the approaches these RHIOs have taken to structure their operations and the strategies they use to provide timely, shared access to patient information. The site also details some of the barriers and challenges that RHIOs typically encounter on their road to functionality.

Collectively, this and other research into RHIOs underscores today's reality that there has not yet been a single organizational structure or strategy for disseminating and sharing patient and financial data across a network of disparate stakeholders that can be considered "best in class." The Agency for Healthcare Research and Quality (AHRQ) reported in January 2006 that while RHIOs have embraced technology, there is wide variation in how RHIOs use technology to facilitate the transfer of patient and financial data throughout their stakeholder organizations.[3] The report also suggests that the interest in participating in RHIOs varies among healthcare organizations. This variability is often tied to concerns about data ownership and the ability to achieve interoperability among disparate clinical information systems to provide shared access to patient and financial information throughout an RHIO network.

After involvement with and review of RHIOs that are both fledgling and fully operational, the authors have determined there are essentially three broad approaches that RHIOs undertake to address these important issues of data ownership and interoperability:

Transactional Model

This strategy is often characterized by the exchange of e-mails and other messaging that delivers both patient and financial information from individual patient encounters to clinicians and caregivers in a RHIO network. This is often a beginning-stage approach that requires little change in the technologies clinicians and caregivers currently use. As such, it is also a stepping-stone to a more integrated strategy that enables larger amounts of patient information—histories, past diagnoses, etc.—to flow through the RHIO network.

Centralized Model

A chief feature of this approach is a central data repository from which clinicians and caregivers in a RHIO network can access and input information about patient encounters—with an eye toward giving all those involved a fuller view of the continuum of care for patients. By its nature, a centralized model triggers the need for interoperability among disparate clinical information systems to enable them to "talk" to each other. At the same time, participants in this RHIO model must also agree on standards for the data they share (i.e., developing uniform terminology and data entry methods for conditions like allergies) so that all clinicians and caregivers know how to interpret and use information that comes from another organization or department within the RHIO network. From a technology perspective, the centralized approach also typically requires an investment in a single vendor or integration provider to build a centralized data repository and make it functional for all stakeholders. This approach also requires concurrence among RHIO stakeholders on who "owns" the data that resides in the repository.

Federated Model

This model is characterized by data-sharing technology that enables RHIO participants to view and share patient information without the creation of a central repository. This technology also enables interoperability among the disparate clinical information systems already in use at participating RHIO organizations, allowing clinicians and caregivers to view patient histories, diagnoses, lab results and other data needed for clinical decision-making in formats with which they are already familiar. Some view this model as a long-term strategy that will speed RHIO development because it allows for the sharing of patient information without the need for creating uniform standards for patient data or addressing the data ownership question. In turn, the elimination of these factors can lead to wider access to and usage of patient data within participating RHIO organizations. In this model, each RHIO organization defines and retains the patient data they need to support clinical decisions and improved patient care.

Overview of Case Studies

The following case studies examine the experiences of two existing RHIOs that use the centralized and federated structural models. The Ann Arbor Area Health Information Exchange RHIO, which represents 4 primary care and specialty practices, 300 physicians and nurse practitioners, and 400,000 patients, uses a centralized model as the foundation for its organization. In 2006, this three-year-old RHIO established itself as a for-profit, limited liability corporation (LLC).

Secondly, the Clalit/Rambam/Sheba RHIO in Israel, which involves a network of 16 hospitals (8,100-plus beds), 1,600 specialized clinics and pharmacies, and 10,000 clinicians, uses a federated model as its foundation. Because of its sheer size and the two-dozen plus clinical information systems in operation across its member organizations, this RHIO adopted a federated architecture as the basis for its data sharing strategy. This RHIO has been operational since 2001 and comprises 2.5 billion individual patient records.

Case Study of a Centralized RHIO Model: Ann Arbor Area Health Information Exchange

Scope of Project

In 2003, recognizing that community-wide electronic health information exchange would improve patient care and help control healthcare delivery costs, a forward-thinking group of physicians in Ann Arbor, Michigan, joined forces to create a RHIO. Ultimately called the Ann Arbor Area Health Information Exchange (A^3HIE), the physicians organized a fledgling electronic medical record program around a community health portal that was easily accessible via the World Wide Web.

A^3HIE comprises four primary care and specialty practices: Integrated Health Associates, Michigan Heart, Huron Gastroenterology, and Michigan Multi-specialty Physicians. It represents 250 physicians and 50 nurse practitioners and serves 400,000 patients—about 75% of the greater Ann Arbor community. The coalition was founded with a simple one-page letter of agreement but, after successfully navigating the first stage of its development, A^3HIE formally established itself in 2006 as a for-profit LLC. The physicians intend eventually to seek nonprofit status for their organization.

Currently, the practices share four specific data sets: patient demographic information, medications, allergies, and current problem and diagnoses lists. Physicians can enter information into their practices' electronic medical record (EMR) system, and relevant details are "pushed" to the central data repository where other partners can access and import it securely.

Mission and Goals

At the heart of the collaboration is a belief that making patient health information readily available to one another electronically achieves two primary goals:

- **Enhancement of quality of care and improvement in patient safety.** Physicians eventually will have an up-to-date patient record at their disposal as they make vital diagnostic and therapeutic decisions. This allows them to take into consideration other care plans and courses of therapy, potential drug interactions, and relevant allergies.

- **Reduction of operational and administrative costs.** Physicians have access to results of lab work and diagnostic tests ordered by colleagues, minimizing the number of duplicative studies performed. In addition, electronic data interchange eliminates paperwork and associated supply, handling and personnel costs.

Management and Physician Leadership

The coalition of physicians that formed A^{3}HIE appointed an administrator in a role that is expanding from part-time (eight hours per week) to full-time status to oversee the RHIO operations. The coalition also established three planning and implementation committees to guide its coordinated activities and build the "centralized" data repository:

- **Development group.** Composed of physicians and information technology (IT) professionals, this committee confers about "big picture" issues such as what types of data would be captured in the central repository and what tools should be developed to make accessing that data as easy as possible.
- **Technology group.** IT representatives from each practice, familiar with their own databases, sit on this committee to tackle the technology challenges—how to create the templates, forms and processes that would facilitate sharing agreed-upon clinical information.
- **Administrative group.** Administrative leaders representing each partner meet frequently to develop the administrative structure allowing the consortium to work smoothly.

Achievements to Date

Two important factors have contributed to the technology achievements of the participants in the A^{3}HIE RHIO. First, the participating physicians shared a collaborative vision for the sharing of patient information that transcended potential pitfalls such as the governing structure for the RHIO organization and enabled agreement on parameters for selecting a single EMR provider. Second, the participating organizations agreed on a phased, practice-focused roll-out that would enable participants to grow into their RHIO participation.

Factors Contributing to Success

Leadership has identified several factors that contributed to the success A^{3}HIE has experienced:

- **Commitment to collaboration.** The partners had a positive relationship before launching A^{3}HIE. Physicians had referred patients among themselves for years, and had abandoned any fears that they would "lose" patients to another practice. In addition, all had connections with St. Joseph Mercy Hospital and the University of Michigan, and shared a similar payor base.
- **Shared technology.** Each practice chose the same EMR system, which means all partners work from similar forms and templates, making it easier to interface with the central repository. The practices began their search for an EMR about the same

time and compared results from product evaluations. Knowing from the onset that they wanted to build a community information exchange, they identified specific features the systems must exhibit, including standard technologies like HL7 and SQL (Standard Query Language), open architecture for flexibility and scalability, and interfaces with diagnostic equipment. Ultimately, each selected NextGen® EMR, from NextGen Healthcare Information Systems.

- **Simple governance structure.** Partners kept governance simple from the beginning, focusing on building an information exchange from the ground up in a manner that would meet each practice's needs. Decisions were made collaboratively, with administrators, physicians and IT professionals contributing to all discussions.
- **Operability over interoperability.** A³HIE emphasized "operability" over "interoperability," taking the time to allow each practice to implement its own EMR successfully before expecting it to participate in the centralized exchange. Each EMR was configured to assist physician workflow at each practice. A³HIE's technology infrastructure—and resulting processes and procedures—were based on what worked at the practice level.
- **Shared commitment and vision.** The 250 physicians comprising A³HIE came together voluntarily and have invested their own intellectual and financial capital to date. In selecting new partners to expand their RHIO (e.g., hospitals, payors, employers, etc.), they will do so for sound clinical and business reasons, not from a commitment borne out of the formation planning.

Addressing Challenges

While A³HIE was able to circumvent many obstacles similar consortiums encounter at start-up, it nevertheless faced several challenges:

- **Patient identification.** Physicians complained that it was difficult to determine whether or not a patient new to their practice had been seen by another partner in the consortium; searching the database to locate an existing record was cumbersome, time-consuming and interfered with their established workflow. To address this, practices now enter three of four specific demographic items when searching for a patient record. When a match is found, the user can simply import select data directly into their own EMR data fields.
- **Patient care continuity.** Physicians requested an alert that would notify them if established patients had been seen by another provider since their last visit. Working with its technology vendor, A³HIE is developing functionality to address this concern. A button will appear when the patient chart is retrieved at the time of the visit, allowing the practice access to the data in the repository.
- **Privacy.** A³HIE struggled with privacy and HIPAA concerns, debating whether patients should be given the choice to opt out of the central repository. It has afforded patients that alternative and has found that most elect to have their medical record included.

Looking Ahead

As it enters the next stage of development, A³HIE has established a number of objectives:

- **Expansion of the coordinated record.** At the top of the list is making additional clinical information available to existing partners—like personal, family and social histories (PFSH).

- **Refinement of the referral/consultation system.** A second priority is to streamline referral and consultation communications so each provider receives comprehensive information quickly.

- **Expansion of the physician partnership.** The consortium is committed to expanding access to other physicians in the community. To that end, A³HIE is currently discussing the ideal balance between primary care providers and specialists, how to configure its governance structure as new partners come on board, and how to add emergency departments that have a vital need for up-to-date patient health information.

- **Capital seed funding.** A³HIE is seeking seed money from local sources and pursuing government grants. Likewise, it will collaborate with St. Joseph Mercy Hospital in Ann Arbor, a nonprofit entity that works with physicians to obtain funding for special initiatives.

- **Financial sustainability.** A³HIE is also exploring a less traditional source of revenue: marketing the information that resides in the A³HIE central repository. The aggregate data relating to specific conditions and diseases, as well as the efficacy of various treatment protocols, represents a valuable resource to entities like disease management firms and pharmaceutical companies who could use the information in clinical studies.

- **Development of a personal health record.** A³HIE is committed to making a personal health record available to the patient through the Web portal and to providing comprehensive records on a memory stick so patients can take their charts with them when they travel.

- **Collaboration with the patient/consumer.** A³HIE will engage the community in the oversight of its activities. By doing so, the consortium will gain significant public credibility, which will lead to its recognition as a respected public healthcare data exchange worthy of future clinical and capital investment.

Over the long term, A³HIE must establish itself as a financially stable enterprise that offers value to a wide range of stakeholders—healthcare providers, patients, payors and employers. In addition, it will need to raise its public profile, educating the Ann Arbor community about how sharing health information enhances the care for all individuals while maintaining the privacy and security of each patient's specific clinical data.

Case Study of a Federated RHIO Model: Clalit/Rambam/Sheba RHIO

Scope of Project

This RHIO formed as leaders of the Clalit HMO and its participating hospitals and clinics recognized the difficulties of clinicians seeing many of the same patients but lacking access to patient information that would inform them of previous visits, diagnoses, and treatment protocols undertaken by clinicians in different clinical settings. The participating providers—Clalit/Rambam/Sheba—represent individual enterprise networks that serve more than 4 million patients through 16 hospitals (>8,100 beds), 400 pharmacies, 1,200 primary care and specialized clinics, and 10,000 clinicians. The RHIO, which has been operational since 2001, comprises 2.5 billion individual healthcare records.

The providers agreed that a more collaborative approach would assist them in overcoming challenges of sharing data that occurred both within the respective organizations (e.g., between individual departments) and between disparate hospitals and community clinics and other care settings.

As with many healthcare organizations, the data sharing problems stemmed from a disparate network of more than 25 clinical information systems that could not "talk" to each other and allow clinicians and caregivers to access the information stored in their individual data repositories.

At the point of care, real-time medical decisions were often based on partial information because complete medical records, spread over disparate storage systems, were not readily accessible. With limited access to information, duplicate and unnecessary tests and procedures occurred and the care cycle was drawn out in relation to gathering sufficient information for proper diagnosis and treatment.

Mission and Goals

The three participating providers in the RHIO all agreed that addressing their respective data sharing challenges in a collaborative manner would yield important outcomes for their organizations and patients. The providers settled on a federated model for their RHIO to provide the interoperability they needed between disparate clinical systems. After establishing a host of prerequisites and goals that a technology solution would need to deliver, the RHIO participants chose dbMotion as their chief technology partner. The technology solution fit with the RHIO's federated architecture and offered a cost-effective and organization-focused approach to ensuring the sharing of patient data across a wide network of providers and enabling autonomy and ownership of patient information at individual institutions.

The RHIO participants established ten goals:

1. **Find an All-Encompassing Technology Solution**

    The providers identified several challenges that served as prerequisites for selecting a technology partner:
    -   Large quantity of legacy, HIS, EMR systems;
    -   Heterogeneous tech environment;
    -   Large volume and size of organizations;
    -   Competing and different needs; and
    -   Finding the right answers to sensitive, complex issues that include ethics, security, privacy, performance, standards, coding systems and more.

2. **Allow Individual RHIO Clinics, Hospitals and Care Facilities to "Own" Their Data**

    This goal was a key reason for opting for the federated RHIO model and selecting dbMotion technology. The architecture of the federated system is based on autonomous units, called 'nodes,' on which the system is installed. Nodes are located at a number of potentially independent healthcare facilities/organizations. This federated network solution logically interconnects healthcare organizations and medical information providers of different types to enable the on-demand formation of virtual patient records, without the need for a central database or the replacing of existing data-storage systems. All information remains at its original location and in its original format, maintained by its original owner (the organization that created it). The system accesses and returns data to the various nodes on the network according to the Unified Medical Schema (UMS), which is a proprietary data-formatting function that allows the standardization and transport of disparate clinical information to/from nodes on the system.

3. **Give Caregivers Access to Patient Data**

    The federated RHIO structure and "nodes-based" technology architecture enable caregivers to access patient data that is securely gathered from all the different sources in the network and merged into an integrated patient record that is displayed to the caregiver at the point of care. When a caregiver at a connected entity wishes to retrieve a patient's clinical information, they log in to their local node via a user-friendly Web-based application authenticated to the local node by local access control and security systems.

    They then input a minimum set of demographic patient information, thus initiating a query. The query is then submitted to the EMPI to identify the whereabouts of clinical data or health information for this patient at the local node as well as at all the other nodes on the network. In cases in which the caregiver already has access to an electronic medical record of some sort, this system will pass the patient and user identification information to the server to facilitate a seamless log-in to the system. The system then returns a set of results that display where data for the patient is located across the network of nodes. The caregiver can simply click on the patient information they wish to see and the system accesses the relevant patient data in the clinical/operational systems or clinical data repository (CDR) at any of the various nodes and returns the information according to a unified medical schema, irrespective of the facility from which it was retrieved.

4. **Provide Real-time Access to Patient Data**

    Given the size and scope of the RHIO, the participating providers required that any data-sharing solution enable real-time access to patient data to ensure caregivers had the most up-to-date view of encounters with patients. The 'nodes' technology enables real-time access by interfacing with disparate clinical systems. (The local HIS systems and hardware platforms were disparate, with more than 25 existing systems (ADT, LIS, ORS, RIS, Pathology, Imaging, etc). These diverse data storage systems could not "talk" to each other, information repositories were isolated, ownership was diverse and there was a lack of interoperability between systems in use.

    In instances where the systems do not allow real-time access, the technology uses an off-line interface that incorporates a physical repository that captures transactions from the various clinical/operations systems and stores them in an intermediary node database. In some cases, for systems that provide data extracts only, batch processing of patient information can be carried out at the off-line physical repository. In either case, data is transformed into the technology vendor's UMS that is consistent across all nodes. The UMS is the data model used by all the system layers. All the nodes are interconnected via a secure network using any supported Wide Area Network (WAN) topology and encryption at both the tunnel (Virtual Private Network-VPN) and data levels.

5. **Address Patient Identification across Multiple Systems**

To identify and link the identities of patients across multiple systems, the technology uses EMPI technology to create a trusted system of records. This technology overcomes duplicate and fragmented records, multiple identifications, transpositions, misspellings, nicknames, aliases, address inconsistencies, and identity misrepresentations to find and link all the records about a person (patient), across disparate systems and data sources. The EMPI integrates and consolidates patient indexes from multiple registration systems into a single index, providing matched patients demographic clusters. Implementation is carried out as follows.

The caregiver enters a request for patient data with demographic information, in line with the search criteria, either using the front-end viewer application or by handshake with the user's existing clinical desktop application (single sign on). This activates the virtual identifier aggregation (VIA) service that communicates with the EMPI. On receipt of the response from the EMPI the VIA service creates a patient identity object that is used by all internal processes as a unique identifier of this patient in the context of the current session.

6. **Integrate Data with Minimal Expense and Frustration**

The RHIO providers selected vendor for its technology solution because of the complex mapping process it uses to effectively tie together disparate patient information without expensive, "hard" interfaces with disparate clinical systems.

The mapping process enables data integration from the disparate data sources, which subsequently feed the proprietary UMS. This process is carried out at each node in the network and is the backbone of the implementation process for each new node added to the network.

The mapping process starts by collecting examples of all the available Legacy message documentation. Then the mapping itself is carried out using UMS mapping tables that provide a framework for the process. Data messages in multiple formats such as HL7(V2.x/3.x), ASCII(text), CCR, Edifact, XML, and more are mapped into the UMS. The full integration process for a node takes from three to six months, depending on the scope of the data for mapping at the node.

From a clinical standpoint, the benefit of this integration approach can be significant for caregivers. For example, a caregiver can use the system to trend lab parameters over time, regardless of the way the original lab result was represented and stored. This rids the caregiver of the challenge of manually comparing individual results from various sources and presents the data in a single view that enables the clinician to efficiently assess the results over time.

7. **Ensure Security of Patient Information.**

The size and scope of the RHIO, and its thousands of clinical caregivers, requires significant protections to ensure the security of patient information throughout the network. The RHIO providers agreed that the federated structure, and the technology's ability to allow individual clinics and facilities to "own" and store data, were key benefits that would aid their efforts to protect patient data from unauthorized access. The system addresses data security as shown in the box.

How Data Security Is Ensured

The security authority provides an interface for connections to all the other system layers. Security Layer Authentication is carried out using each organization's authentication system(s) so that information about users and credentials are maintained by the organization/entity.

The mechanism involves the UPO (user principal object), a token created when user credentials are authenticated. This token is passed along with all requests submitted to the different layers, as well as to remote nodes and contains information regarding the identity of the user.

Authorization is defined as the process of resolving a user's entitlements with the permissions configured to control access to a resource. The technology uses a role-based access control (RBAC) model for managing users and permissions that enables the healthcare organization's security administrators to configure and manage user access rights to the information and services provided. This model assigns users and groups to predefined roles associated with the permissions they require to do their jobs.

As indicated above, the decentralized architecture simplifies the handling of patient privacy as well as ownership and control of information. The UPO is created on the spot and is typically configured to dissipate after use, so policy changes can be quickly implemented. The decision, for example, to stop sharing a specific type of patient information requires no more than a simple change in definitions and this data will no longer be transferred. There is no need to erase the data from various databases because it is simply not stored anywhere other than in its original location. Security remains maximal, as each organization remains responsible for its own data. This limits risk and provides for more flexibility

---

8. **Minimize Clinical Workflow Disruption Caused by Technology**

    The nodes-based architecture of the federated model allows caregivers the opportunity to access and view patient data they request on the systems they are accustomed to using. This approach alleviates concerns about "change" among clinicians and caregivers and minimizes disruptions to their workflows.

9. **Ensure System Reliability**

    With federated network architecture, if for any reason, one node is down or disconnected from the network, system performance is not affected and data continues to flow between the active nodes. This means that the end-user can rely on the network even if for some reason one of the nodes is not connected. The clinician or end-user, even if he/she is located at a remote clinic, can always see, using the front-end viewing application, from which nodes information has reached him/her as well as which (if any) nodes are down.

10. **Allow for System Scalability**

    As the RHIO adds additional partners and functionality, it wanted to be sure the system allowed for scalability to accommodate changing needs. The technology addresses scalability as follows:

    - **Network.** The federated network architecture provides for the addition or removal of nodes in a flexible and modular manner.

- **Clinical domains.** Initial implementation may involve certain clinical domains only. In the course of time, additional domains can be incorporated. For example, for the RHIO covered by this case study, initial implementation was for the Labs Domain only and additional domains were added subsequently without interfering with the ongoing operation of the system.
- **New users.** End user access is accomplished using a Web-based application. This means that end-users can be added either at the local node, or at any geographical location where there is a connection to the Internet and a Web browser. All that is required is for the new clinician or end-user to be authenticated in the system with a defined permissions level that establishes the data he is authorized to view.

Management and Physician Leadership

The RHIO began in 2000 with a joint effort headed by Clalit's CEO, Dr. Yitzchak Peterburg, who is known as an early adopter of technology and a leader interested in using technology to improve organization performance.

The formation of the RHIO then took on two broad phases, the implementation of data-sharing at Clalit-member organizations, followed by the addition of other organizations. The start of implementation at Clalit began with the formation of a Minimal Data Set Committee (MDS), which was comprised of physicians and leaders from Clalit's provider network.

Next, individual organizations such as Sheba Medical Center then used the Clalit template to implement the technology and data-sharing at their own organizations, with the goal of connecting to the Clalit network. Once the connectivity occurred, each individual organization then established its own management committee that handles ongoing operational issues. Following is a breakdown of each of these developmental and operational phases.

- **MDS Committee.** This group established a primary goal: "To manage our customer's health, in real-time, maintaining continuity of care in a disjointed and distributed environment." The MDS's initial charge was to create a universally accepted data set that all clinicians and caregivers could use in their patient-centric approach to care. The committee established a goal that retrieval of patient information must occur under 10 seconds. The MDS committee researched potential partners and was instrumental in choosing the technology partner for an enterprise-wide solution.
- **Local pilots.** Clalit's CEO and CIO led an initiative at the HMO's largest tertiary hospital, Soroka Hospital, to implement a pilot of the technology that would serve as a template for other organizations interested in joining the RHIO. The pilot project used the outcomes of the MDS Committee's work and technology to successfully connect acute, primary and ambulatory care departments. The success of this initiative, which used a federated architecture that allowed individual departments to "own" their data, led to Clalit's decision to expand the network on an enterprise-wide scale.
- **Network roll-out.** As Clalit expanded the roll-out of technology and federated architecture model to all organizations, it decided to first go to participating hospitals and then to clinics. At each affiliate organization, the chief medical officer

(CMO) took the lead in implementing the solution. The CMO then established a steering committee, ethics committee, users committee and implementation committee to manage the implementation at individual hospitals and clinics. For example, the ethics committee at each organization would establish the profiles (resident, physician, lab worker, nurse, etc.) and authentications needed to ensure secure sharing of patient data. The implementation committee would then oversee the adoption of the ethics committee's recommendations.

As Clalit's succeeded in its efforts to provide real-time data sharing among its participating organizations, Clalit's leaders then began work to join the Chaim Sheba Medical Center and the Rambam Medical Center. Both organizations adopted and used the implementation models Clalit had established. The prior success helped speed the development of the RHIO network. For example, the connection between Clalit and Sheba Medical Center took only two months.

- **Ongoing management.** Each organization within the RHIO has followed a model of tiered support to enable the ongoing, efficient use of the technology and ensure the technology and patient data access adjusts as clinical needs change. For example, each hospital has a first-tier referral level if operational issues arise. At Clalit headquarters, a second-tier level of support and management works with individual RHIO organizations to make adjustments to patient records and handle change requests. A third tier of support comes from the technology partner, which monitors the system's usage and responds to any needed changes or adjustments. In addition, a half-FTE position provides training and use of the system throughout the RHIO organizations.

At the organization level, each organization sets up its own support structure. For example, the CIOs at Rambam and Sheba medical centers manage the data-sharing initiative. At Clalit, two FTEs in the MIS department oversee the data sharing technology and ongoing usage.

Achievements to Date

Perhaps the largest achievement for the RHIO would be its full operation and use across a RHIO network that consists of 16 hospitals, 1,200 clinics and a host of other affiliated labs, pharmacies and other organizations. On an anecdotal level, executives, physicians and caregivers at individual organizations within the RHIO report greater patient care quality, safety, satisfaction and outcomes. Many are also pleased at the consistent performance of patient data retrieval that occurs in less than 10 seconds. Some examples of these anecdotal results:

- **Fewer duplicate and unnecessary tests.** The data sharing enables clinicians to look up previous tests and results to determine to make more precise diagnoses on a patient's immediate condition.
- **Lower probability of medical errors.** Real time access to patient data includes medications prescribed by anyone within the network, thereby reducing the need for potential drug interactions.
- **Shorter care cycles.** Clinicians report the access to patient data provides a clearer understanding of a patient's condition and thereby reduces the potential for admissions and readmissions. Clinicians also say the quick retrieval of patient

information enables them to spend more qualitative time with patients, which also aids their ability to correctly diagnose and treat a patient's condition.

- **Proactive care.** The messaging functionality of the system, as well as the access it provides to patient data about past hospitalizations and treatments, enables clinicians to dialogue with other caregivers to more effectively manage the continuum of care for patients. This dynamic is especially true between acute and community care settings.

Factors Contributing to Success

A multitude of factors have contributed to the success of the RHIO—from the technology-friendly vision of leadership to the dedication of clinicians and others involved in the necessary committee work to create a structure and implementation plan to enable the roll-out of the technology and spur collaboration among disparate acute and community care settings.

   On a more granular level, the success of this RHIO also owes to some of the early and ongoing decisions that organizers made to aid the implementation. Several key factors that contributed to this RHIO's success include:

- **Commitment to improved patient care.** From its earliest stage, the architects and organizers of the RHIO all viewed the data sharing initiative as a pathway to improved patient care—a mindset that continues to guide the management of the RHIO network.
- **Adoption of the federated architecture.** The combination of the federated architecture and the technology helped alleviate parochial concerns such as data ownership and security that have undermined RHIO initiatives elsewhere. Similarly, the flexibility of the structure and technology solution helped alleviate concerns about potential cost and clinical workflow disruption. In addition, the ability of the technology to work on systems that clinicians are accustomed to using has greatly aided the usage levels among clinicians and caregivers.
- **Clinician involvement.** Through its use of committees at participating organizations, the RHIO organizers tapped all stakeholders in the administrative and clinical settings of disparate organizations to garner their input and buy-in for the adoption and implementation of the data sharing technology. This approach also helped underscore the RHIO's central purpose of improving patient care quality.
- **Ongoing, decentralized management.** The ability of individual organizations within the RHIO to adjust the patient data they access and use to fit their changing clinical needs is a key benefit. In addition, the support mechanisms at the individual organization, Clalit's headquarters and the technology partner's support team engender ongoing confidence and trust in the data-sharing system among users.

Addressing Challenges

Perhaps the foremost challenges for the RHIO's formation rested on the ability of a technology solution to enable disparate clinical systems to "talk" to one another and enable clinicians and caregivers to access the information most important for their individual practices and clinical settings. The RHIO organizers adopted the federated architecture and technology because of the combined ability they promised to address this fundamental hurdle to real-time access to patient data across a disparate network of organizations and clinical systems. A second challenge occurred after the RHIO was functioning and clinicians and caregivers wanted to achieve greater collaboration of care.

Tying Disparate Systems Together

The architecture of the technology accomplishes this important task by using a series of layers that enable the movement and access to data across the RHIO network:

- **Data integration layer.** The data integration layer is responsible for data fetching from existing legacy systems, entry into the system and their initial transformation into the unified medical schema. This transformation means that irrespective of the source or source format, all data entering into the network will be in the unified medical schema format only. This involves establishing a data communication channel between existing systems and the system network.

- **Data layer.** The data layer is responsible for the storage of data retrieved in its clinical data repository, designed to manage patient information retrieved by the integration layer from distributed heterogeneous and dynamic data sources in such a way that the disparate data sources appear as one database. This means that access to data through the solution network is transparent—the original data source is not exposed. This is made possible by the fact that all data in the CDR is stored according to technology partner's proprietary unified medical schema.

- **Communication and transportation layers.** The communication layer is responsible for the collection of clinical data from the various nodes defined in the system. Clinical data at a remote node is stored in the remote node data layer, typically in a CDR. The data collection is accomplished using proprietary communication protocols and the data is stored initially in temporary storage located at the node that initiated the request, ready to be incorporated into the creation of a virtual patient object (VPO), the patient-centric data object used to contain and mobilize the integrated patient information in a session. To actually transport the data, the communication layer uses the transport layer infrastructure of communication pipelines that enable additional processing such as encryption and decryption that enhance security in transit.

- **Business layer.** The business layer deals with the transformation of raw data accumulated by the communication layer, often with input from external Web services, into an understandable response to the request initiator. Typically, the request initiator is the presentation layer, although the technology can support other external data consumers. This transformation is carried out by the execution of various business processes using a number of business services. The technology provides considerable added value to the raw data by virtue of these processes. The response is returned to the presentation layer, (or other consumer), as the VPO can be delivered in diverse formats, depending on the consumer requirements. The VPO encapsulates all the available data relevant to the patient and the request. This layer effectively constitutes the "brain" behind most of the processes of information sharing between the various organizations or data providers and the functions of this layer in each node and in the network as a whole are manifold.

- **Presentation layer.** The presentation layer is the top layer of the multi-layer system and is also known as the front-end. This layer provides the end user with a built-in user interface. Clinical data, processed in the business layer, is displayed using a Web-based application that can be modified according to customer requirements. This enables fast access for a user to the relevant data from the VPO, with considerable flexibility for processing the data presented.

- **Security layer.** The security layer, of prime importance in the multi-layer technology, defines the aggregate of safeguards, both technical and administrative, that prevent prohibited access to this ePHI (electronically Protected Health Information) by unauthorized parties, both among internal users and users outside enterprise boundaries. These safeguards are implemented via a number of sub-systems, each dealing with a different aspect of information security.
- **Management layer.** The operational management layer incorporates applications (tools) that enable the management of subsystems, modules and services. Management involves operation, configuration, testing and monitoring.
- **System layer.** The system layer provides the basis for the system's software development kit and incorporates all the core components required for developers working with the different system layers. These include libraries, and frameworks or low-level environments.

Enabling Greater Clinician Collaboration

After two years of operation, clinicians among the RHIO organizations sought to incorporate messaging into the VPO to allow for enhanced communication. The technology easily allowed the addition of this functionality, which has gained widespread use among clinicians and caregivers. In 2003, the RHIO logged more than 100,000 messages between clinicians and caregivers.

Looking Ahead

The RHIO has several initiatives underway that will aid its goal of providing greater access to patient data and improving patient care on a broader scale, including:

- Developing a national patient information network. The RHIO's success has contributed to an effort in Israel to develop a national information network that would allow any clinician or caregiver in the country to access information about a given patient. The government's initial efforts indicate it is interested in using the federated architecture that has proven successful at the RHIO.

- Allowing at-home access to patient information. Discussions are underway to develop external access for both patients and caregivers to clinical information so both can take a more active role in the care and treatment to patients at their homes.

References

1. States Getting Connected: Quality and Safety Driving Health IT Planning in a Majority of the States in the United States. eHI Issue Brief. July, 2006. Available at www.ehealthinitiative.org/assets/documents/eHI2006ReportonStateActivities.pdf.
2. HIT Dashboard. HIMSS. Available at www.hitdashboard.com.
3. Evolution of State Health Information Exchange: A Study of Vision, Strategy, and Progress. Agency for Healthcare Research and Quality. January, 2006. Available at www.avalerehealth.net/research/docs/State_based_Health_Information_Exchange_Final_Report.pdf.

CHAPTER 7

Practical Use Cases: The Possibilities of Administrative and Clinical Data Exchange

David S. Szabo and Elaine A. Blechman, PhD

Regional health information organizations (RHIOs) have the challenging task of satisfying the diverse business and personal communication requirements of government and healthcare enterprises and of individual healthcare consumers. Technology development is, at best, driven by use cases or scenarios that articulate, in non-technical language, how a system should interact with end users to achieve their valued goals. Satisfying the needs of end users is the "acid test" for measuring the utility of a RHIO. Information technology should advance the goals of both healthcare providers and individual healthcare recipients and other relevant stakeholders. Ultimately, the interests of individual patients must be paramount, because the quality of healthcare outcomes is often a life-or-death matter. This chapter is intended to illustrate a few current and potential uses of RHIOs, and their application to the improvement of healthcare delivery.

By reviewing current and possible uses of administrative and clinical data exchange, our understanding of technology, governance, privacy, security and sustainability of RHIOs can move from a theoretical exercise to practical problem solving. In other words, by understanding the possibilities of what a RHIO can do, we will have a better grasp on how to build, operate and sustain them.

Each use case is accompanied by a specific example of a RHIO or data exchange project. However, this chapter does not pretend to comprehensively survey of RHIO activity around the U.S. Instead, a few examples of actual RHIO implementations are provided so that the reader can see varying approaches to reaching the goal of comprehensive clinical data exchange within a community or region.

Why Have a Data Exchange Organization at All?

RHIOs are intended to facilitate communication of healthcare information, including both administrative information, such as claims, and clinical information, such as prescription histories, lab results and images. This suggests a question: why have organizations at all? If professionals and organizations want to communicate, why can't they just establish point-to-point, bilateral communication of administrative and clinical data and thereby achieve their objective?

Of course, point-to-point communication is possible and often is very valuable. However, establishing point-to-point communication with many trading partners can be difficult. Differences in technology and business processes among trading partners can greatly increase the difficulty and cost of establishing and managing many point-to-point connections. This is especially true when trading partners want to make their information systems highly interoperable, so that messages can be received and appropriately acted upon with a minimum of human intervention and review. A RHIO can serve as a "bridge" between otherwise isolated information systems, using a variety of technical and business approaches to make communication between disparate enterprises easier and more useful.

A more fundamental reason for establishing a RHIO is that the greatest benefits of administrative and clinical data interchange can be realized only if a critical mass of trading partners participates in the interchange. Administrative electronic data interchange, such as electronic handling of claims and referral authorizations, can reduce cost, but only if large numbers of transactions can be handled in a standardized, routine way with a minimum of errors and re-work. Such standardization and the resulting cost savings can be realized if, and only if, a high percentage of the trading partners in a market or community adopt interoperable information systems and business processes. This network effect can increase the value of data exchange in a dramatic fashion.

The advantages of broad interoperability for clinical data exchange can also readily be appreciated. Patients may have clinical encounters in many settings, with a variety of providers. The healthcare delivery system is highly fragmented, especially the system for delivery of ambulatory care. However, information needed for one particular encounter (such as pharmacy history or information on prior tests and treatments) may not be readily available at the point of care, particularly in an emergency or during an encounter with a provider who is new to the patient. The value of clinical data exchange is in part a function of its ability to capture both information about a high percentage of patients, and a significant portion of the meaningful clinical information about each such patient.

Building systems that can access meaningful information about a large numbers of patients may require coordination among many providers and payors, each with its own information systems and business processes. Success might require the use of at least some common technology, common consultants, common vendors, or common business processes. A RHIO can serve as a forum where this level of coordination and development can take place.

The following sections of this chapter will illustrate possible "use cases" for the application of interoperable health information technology. The discussion will not be technical, but will focus on the role of the RHIO or other organization on facilitating the exchange of administrative and clinical information.

Facilitating EDI for Administrative Transactions

One of the first uses of a RHIO was for facilitating electronic data interchange (EDI) of administrative transactions between health plans and healthcare providers. The administrative simplification provisions of HIPAA authorized the Secretary of Health and Human Services (HHS) to adopt eight "standard transactions" for EDI between health care providers, health plans and health care clearinghouses, and by regulation to adopt standard codes, content and formats for the standard electronic transactions.

The HIPAA standard transaction rules were intended to reduce the cost of processing routine administrative transactions such as claims, remittances, referral authorizations and health plan enrollment. However, many providers found that implementation of EDI with numerous trading partners was expensive and/or unwieldy. Often, the most practical way for providers to implement the standard transactions was through a healthcare clearinghouse, sometime paying a fee for each and every transaction received or transmitted.

Administrative RHIOs were formed to enable health plans and healthcare providers to collaborate on EDI so as to standardize their information technology practices and reduce the cost of processing routine transactions. Examples of RHIOs formed around administrative transactions include the Utah Health Information Network (UHIN) and the New England Healthcare EDI Network (NEHEN).

Using Payor Claims Data to Reduce Medical Errors in the Hospital Emergency Department

Physicians and other clinicians working in hospital emergency departments often treat patients with little or no information about their medical history or current medications. When the patient cannot communicate this information to the physician, the danger of medical errors is obvious.

A number of organizations have recognized this problem, and several projects have been initiated to use existing information resources to provide better information to the point of care. In particular, a number of projects have used claims data to improve healthcare delivery.

Providers tend to be skeptical of the completeness and value of claims information, but claims data has some advantages. Most importantly, claims databases are ubiquitous; claims are probably the most highly available, highly automated form of healthcare information. While far from providing a complete view of the patient's medical history, they are longitudinal, and aggregate information from many providers with respect to any particular patient (member).

There are several sources of claims and related information: health plan claims data and pharmacy benefit managers' databases of pharmacy claims and related information are two prominent examples. Each of these had been tapped for information related to the point of care.

The MEDS-INFO ED pilot project operated in Massachusetts by MA, Simplifying Healthcare Among Regional Entities (MA-SHARE), used e-prescribing technology to connect five hospital emergency rooms to databases maintained by pharmacy benefit managers, managed care plans and the Massachusetts Medicaid program. The application allowed emergency room personnel to look up prescription drug history information for patients covered by any one of seven health plans within minutes and have that information aggregated into a report for delivery to clinical personnel.

Similarly, software that uses health plan claims from payors to create a clinical summary for use in the hospital emergency department is available. The clinical summary uses laboratory, pharmacy, medical and hospital claims information to create a simple report that highlights recent treatments and test results. Emergency room personnel use these summary reports to quickly orient them with respect to the patient's history and can use the clinical summary.

An insurer in Pennsylvania currently is using this type of system to provide information to a large hospital emergency department. Its participants hope to expand it by creating a RHIO that will access data from multiple health plans for use by many emergency departments.

The Hurricane Katrina disaster led to widespread disruption in healthcare delivery in the Gulf Coast region in 2005. As hurricane victims from Louisiana, Mississippi, and elsewhere were relocated, many of them were forced to see healthcare providers who did not know them, with no access to existing medical records.

One response to this disaster was KatrinaHealth.org, a secure Web-based information service that used pharmacy benefit claims data and retail pharmacy data to provide drug history information about survivors to physicians and hospitals around the country. Both KatrinaHealth and MEDSINFO ED took advantage of specialized data switches for locating and retrieving pharmacy and claims data.

Using a Federated Record Locator Service to Link EMR Systems for Primary and Specialty Physician Care

Electronic medical records (EMRs) are becoming more common in provider settings. As EMR systems proliferate, they can become sources of detailed and useful information, but that information may not be available at the point of care when needed. One of the key reasons for the formation of RHIOs is to link these systems in appropriate ways to facilitate care.

One possible solution is the record locator service subscribed to by many healthcare providers. A record locator service using an electronic master patient index can allow an authorized user to locate data without accumulating information in a central database. Under some models, the record locator would use demographic information to identify a unique individual, and then report to the user all locations having records about that individual. The user could then either request that the source transmit information to the user. In other models under consideration, the record locator service would allow the authorized user to "pull" information about the patient from data sources, without actually having to contact the source for permission.

MA-SHARE is currently developing a record locator service that could link many providers' health information systems together in just this way.

Linking Hospital Information Systems for Continuity of Care

Patients may be admitted for care at one hospital shortly after being treated at another institution. This may arise in cases of medical emergency or trauma, where chronic conditions are present, or it may be the result of a referral from a community institution to a tertiary care center. A RHIO could facilitate the transmission of health information among hospitals so that emergency room physicians, specialists and consultants could have ready access to a patient's history of treatment, avoid duplicate tests and avoid medical errors.

Seeing this opportunity, 16 hospitals serving western North Carolina, all members of the Western North Carolina Health Network, have explored options to securely and efficiently exchange electronic patient medical information among the region's healthcare providers. With a long-term goal of allowing every resident of the western North Carolina region to have a longitudinal electronic medical record, they worked to implement a near-term goal of allowing the secure exchange of electronic patient information drawn from the region's 16 hospitals. The hospitals agreed on two key parameters for the project: There would be no central data repository or data warehouse to store patient data, and the project must have the ability to connect with any health information system and be "technology neutral."

The Western North Carolina Health Network is in the process of implementing a federated information system that allows authorized physicians and clinicians to view a patient's electronic records from all 16 participating hospital systems. Upon request, the system searches all of the hospitals' information systems for a patient's records and collates them in a standardized format in real time.

Clinicians can access the records through any Internet-connected device. In future phases, authorized users will be able to access electronic records from physician offices, health departments, clinics and other healthcare providers to create a longitudinal view of the patient's medical history.

Physicians in Cincinnati, Ohio, have access to clinical laboratory results, radiology reports and other clinical data from 17 regional hospitals. Called HealthBridge, the system offers area physicians a common portal and clinical messaging service, providing access to data from each of the participating hospitals. Rather than building a community database, the HealthBridge system uses standards-based communication to allow physicians to securely request and receive clinical messages from each of the participating hospitals. Each hospital maintains control over its own clinical data but allows the HealthBridge system to access data using a community patient index. HealthBridge then provides one point of connection for all participating physicians.

Combining a Hosted EMR with a Health Information Exchange

Another approach to enabling clinical data exchange is to combine a hosted physician EMR with a data repository. Each participating physician group would have access to its own EMR system, with the capability of accessing clinical information from a variety of hospitals, laboratories, imaging centers and other providers. The RHIO would host both the EMR and the data repository.

This model has been implemented by the Michiana Health Information network in South Bend, Indiana. Partnering with a major EMR vendor, the Michiana Network provides health information exchange services for participating physician groups with 15 data sources and is implementing the hosted EMR in physician offices.

Using a Hosted PHR System to Coordinate Long-Term Care for the Elderly and Persons with Disabilities and Chronic Illnesses

One out of five Americans over age five has a chronic illness or disability and requires long-term care services from multiple health and human service providers. Fragmented storage of individuals' medical records in paper and electronic files prevents accountable and effective coordination of long-term care services across healthcare providers and organizations that are unrelated except for shared patients. For patients, the outcomes of uncoordinated care are fraught with needless mistakes, often of poor quality, and sometimes outright harmful. For communities, the outcomes of uncoordinated care are wasteful duplication of services, spiraling costs, and reduced resources for care of the neediest individuals.

RHIOs supported solely by interoperable provider-controlled electronic health records (EHRs) are well prepared to deliver ambulatory care to young and healthy members and ill-prepared to coordinate long-term care for elderly, disabled, and chronically ill members. In the acute phase of a chronic illness, when patients are first diagnosed and treated, multiple physician specialists are involved who are likely to have access to EHRs. In the post-acute phase, patients receive about 85% of their long-term care services from family caregivers, who lack access to provider-controlled EHRs. Most of the remainder of long-term care is supplied by non-physician providers, such as home health aides or nursing home attendants, who also lack access to provider-controlled EHRs. In sum, the prevailing architecture of RHIO-supportive health information technology, with its exclusive reliance on communication among interoperable, provider-controlled EHRs, is incompatible with the long-term care needs of about 40% of Americans, the 20% who require long-term care and the 20% who are family caregivers to chronically ill and disabled relatives.

Ultimately, RHIOs will need comprehensive health information technologies if they are to give equal consideration to the needs of all members including those who are young and healthy and those who are elderly and consumers of long-term care. Such an alternative HIT model involves communication among interoperable, provider-controlled EHRs and interoperable, consumer-controlled personal health record systems (PHRs). Young and healthy individuals would have several records in their various providers' EHRs. Long-term care recipients would have several provider-controlled EHR records and would also have one comprehensive, longitudinal PHR with privileges that they or their family caregivers administer and that integrates care-related information from diverse sources including EHRs. Long-term care recipients or their family caregivers would administer privileges on PHRs so as to give necessary access to providers involved in coordinated care plans and to authorize the automated standards-based exchange of information with trusted providers' EHRs, via a mechanism such as a continuity of care record (CCR).

An online PHR system, hosted by the RHIO or outsourced to a software services provider, would enable patients, family caregivers, and authorized providers to control role-, relationship-, and content-specific access to their PHRs from any location at any time. EHR-deprived providers could coordinate their delivery of services with EHR-equipped providers via the individual's PHR. Until such time as all health and human service providers employ EHRs, this solution benefits not only long-term care recipients but RHIOs that would otherwise be required to subsidize EHR acquisition by member providers who are unable to make a substantial capital investment.

Prosocial Applications, Inc. of Boulder, Colorado, hosts a patent-pending, online, interoperable, consumer-controlled PHR system (Caregiver Alliance Web Services™). The Boulder community was interested in a system that has the functionality required by a RHIO that, as described above, gives equal emphasis to healthy members and to members who are long-term care recipients. The PHR system is deployed for a variety of community-based long-term care coordination purposes and will soon be distributed to 10,000 frail elderly residents of the community. Paralleling the rollout of Caregiver PHRs will be research conducted at the University of Colorado evaluating the role of PHRs in the bottom-up emergence of a RHIO with a unique emphasis on long-term care.

Using a Data Warehouse to Store Protected Health Information for an Entire Community

A record locator service is based on the premise that each healthcare enterprise will continue to maintain its own record system, and that the service would locate and possibly aggregate information on an ad hoc basis. Sometimes enterprises that do not routinely store and aggregate certain health information that may be transactional in nature may deploy local clinical data repositories to facilitate longitudinal informational location. An entirely different approach involves providers, payors and other healthcare entities in the community storing information in a community data warehouse. In principle, a community data warehouse could provide information at the point of care, and also aggregate information for clinical, quality improvement research, public health, bio-surveillance and other authorized purposes.

A community data warehouse may have to interoperate with a wide variety of enterprise systems, and also could support personal health records systems and patient data portals.

An example of a community data warehouse in development is the Louisville Health Information Exchange, Inc. or "LOUHIE." LOUHIE was organized to implement the eHealthTrust™ model for the Louisville, Kentucky area. This model contemplates a large data warehouse whose use is ultimately controlled by patients whose data is stored in the warehouse, with data contributed by providers and others. Once mature, the data warehouse could support clinical care and a wide variety of other activities, including research and public health.

The Indiana Health Information Exchange and the Regenstrief Institute in Indianapolis aim to improve emergency room care and are already using a more limited data warehouse. The Indiana Network for Patient Care has improved emergency care by employing a system of clinical messaging, linking many disparate providers in the Indianapolis area. The Network uses a federated information repository to make patient information available at the point of care for emergency department physicians. This is part of the Exchange's broader clinical messaging service, which delivers clinical reports to the providers electronically, reducing costs for the healthcare data provider and improving efficiency and usability for the recipient. The healthcare data providers send clinical reports to the Exchange electronically, and the Exchange converts them into a consistent report format and delivers them to the point of care.

While the federated record locator service and the community data warehouse may seem like opposite extremes, both models might work together in a community. For example the Massachusetts eHealth Collaborative is providing electronic medical records to physicians in three Massachusetts communities. The Collaborative plans to use a record locator service to link the practice's EMRs together in each community, so that any physician in a community can locate patient data. However, the Collaborative also plans to build a data warehouse for healthcare operations, quality improvement, public health and research purposes. Thus, the federated, decentralized approach to clinical data exchange will be supported by a data warehouse designed to meet specific needs.

Governance Issues Survey Tool

Initial Questionnaire

1. Why are you participating in the effort to organize a regional health information exchange?

2. What do you view as the major objectives and/or gains to be achieved by a regional health information exchange?

3. What are likely to be the key issues for you and your organization's involvement in or use of such an exchange in the next 1, 5, and 10 years (e.g., budget, membership, growth, other)?

4. Which set(s) of decision makers (by function) need to be involved in decisions around the exchange within your organization?
   - During the organizational period?
   - During the operational period?

5. Whom do you believe should participate in the exchange's governance structure and why? Who in your organization would identify these participants and by what process would they do so?

6. Which entities or types of entities should participate in the exchange (e.g., health plans, hospitals, physician offices, community clinics, others)? When should they be allowed to become a participant in the exchange?

7. What should be the overall mission and purpose of the exchange's governing body (e.g., budget, membership, other)?

8. What are the top three priority issues that the exchange's governing body should address in early formation, and why (e.g., funding, growth, expansion of representation, other)?

9. What expectations do you have with respect to any financial commitment that your organization would make to develop and maintain the exchange's governing body?

10. What barriers to participation in the exchange and/or to representation on exchange's governing body do you believe face your organization?

Follow-Up Interview Guide

Costs

1. How do you believe the financial commitment should be determined for those who participate in the exchange and/or its governing body (i.e., methodology)?
2. Are there any financing arrangements with which you are familiar and that might be recommended for the exchange?
3. Once the exchange is operational, there will be ongoing costs related to maintenance, equipment upgrades and other shared expenses. How do you believe these costs should be apportioned across participating entities?
4. Should there be some financial accommodation for certain entities wishing to participate (e.g., based on size or other factors)?

Expanded Participation

1. Ultimately, the exchange may expand its scope. How do you think new participants should be added to the exchange's governance structure?
2. What criteria, if any, do you believe should be used to determine whether one is eligible to participate in the exchange's governance?
3. Do you believe the exchange will have to interface with any statewide or regional organizations, and why?
4. Is there a current mechanism used by your organization to participate in associations such as the exchange? Does this process differ if the participation requires a financial commitment?

Organization Membership

Note: "Members" means the organizations or individuals with respect to an organization that establish and maintain the governance structure, may have certain ultimate decision-making powers and may have rights with respect to assets of the organization upon dissolution.

1. What should be the qualifications to become and remain a member of the exchange?
2. Should there be classes of members with different rights (e.g., founding members, governmental entities, nonprofit providers, individuals, etc.)?
3. If there are classes, how should their powers and responsibilities be different?
4. How should members be selected and admitted?
5. Should members be permitted to withdraw from membership?
6. Should some members be permanent? If so, please give examples.
7. What obligations to the organization should members have (e.g., financial, participation in governance)?

Governing Body Membership

Note: "Governing Body" means a group of individuals with ultimate authority for the management of the affairs of the exchange.

1. Who should select the members of the exchange's governing body?
2. What should be the qualifications for membership on the governing body?
3. Should some actions require a special governing body approval process (e.g., super-majority vote, or vote of specific governing body members)? Can you give some examples (e.g., financial matters, entering into material contracts, etc.)?

Officers

1. Which officers (e.g., chair of the governing body, CEO, CFO) should be volunteers (i.e., unpaid)?
2. Which officers should be compensated executives?

Advisory Bodies

Should the Governing Body have advisory bodies?

- On what subjects?
- Drawing from what perspectives?

Other

1. Do you have any preference regarding whether the entity governing the exchange should be an existing entity or a new entity?
2. Are there any governance arrangements that you are familiar with that might be recommended for the exchange?

RHIO Entity and Governance Objectives and Principles

I.   Overall RHIO Objectives
   A. With respect to form of entity for the RHIO, the planning group intends to establish a plan for a new organization that will
      1.   Be independent
      2.   Be self-governing
      3.   Be self-financing
      4.   Have as its mission
          • [insert RHIO purposes]
II. Entity Objectives
   A. The RHIO entity will be neutral to the interests of the various RHIO customers.
   B. The form of entity will
      1.   Permit the acquisition of the RHIO software applications and equipment
      2.   Be perpetual
      3.   Be tax-exempt to the maximum extent possible
      4.   Be qualified to receive grants
      5.   Have a non-equity holding Membership
      6.   Permit Membership to appoint Directors
   C. The RHIO entity will not be an extension or "creature" of governments
III. Governance Principles
   A. Membership
      1.   "Membership" means the collective entities and individuals that are authorized to establish and maintain the governance structure of the RHIO entity and may have certain ultimate decision-making powers.
      2.   All constituencies will be represented through classes of membership.
      3.   Primary stakeholders will have a major voice.

    4. The Membership will elect the majority of the governing body.

    5. Membership will grow and change to reflect growth and change RHIO customers and in the uses of RHIO products.

B. Governing body

    1. "Governing body" means the group of individuals with ultimate authority for the management of the affairs of the RHIO entity.

    2. The governing body will

       a. Appoint and direct the RHIO entity officers

       b. Establish and oversee implementation of policies regarding:

          i. RHIO product development

          ii. RHIO standardization

          iii. Fees and charges

          iv. Vendor arrangements

       c. Oversee financial performance

       d. Appoint the independent auditors

       e. Accommodate membership composition, growth and change

    3. Directors will be reflective in part of the RHIO customers.

    4. A significant number of directors will be independent; the governing body and the membership shall establish a common definition of "independence" (i.e., relationship to vendors, RHIO customers, funding sources).

    5. Directors will represent diverse backgrounds and necessary skills.

    6. Management will be represented on the governing body.

    7. [Founders] will select some members of the governing body.

    8. Directors will be fiduciaries of the RHIO entity and not representatives of RHIO customers or other affiliations.

    9. The governing body will adopt written statements of its governance principles and code of conduct and regularly re-evaluate them.

    10. The governing body will establish written performance criteria and periodically review governing body performance against those criteria.

    11. The governing body will receive input from Advisory Boards of RHIO constituents (e.g., RHIO customers, funding agencies, healthcare providers, regional interests, enrollees).

    12. Directors will

       a. Have staggered terms

       b. Have term limits

       c. Serve without compensation

    13. The governing body chair will be independent of management.

    14. The governing body will meet without management at least once per year.

    15. Audit, nomination, management evaluation, compliance and ethics functions will be carried out by non-management directors and committees supported by management.

    16. The director nominating function will address

       a. Competing time commitments

       b. Continuing director tenure

       c. Openness to new ideas

      d. Willingness to critically re-examine the status quo

      e. Effective board size

      f. Qualification for re-nomination based on individual behavior expectations (e.g., attendance, preparedness, participation, candor)

      g. The input of the membership

C. Officers

  1. The CEO will

      a. Provide management of day-to-day operations of the RHIO entity

      b. Recommend policy and strategic direction of the RHIO entity for consideration by the governing body

      c. Be spokesperson for the RHIO entity

      d. Be a compensated executive

  2. The governing body chair will

      a. Conduct all meetings of the governing body and the membership

      b. Oversee preparation of governing body and committee agendas

      c. Define the quality, quantity and timeliness of the flow of information between management and the governing body

      d. Approve consultants who report directly to the governing body

      e. Interview candidates for nomination as a director

      f. Oversee development and revision of governance guidelines

      g. Evaluate the CEO's performance

      h. Recommend the composition of governing body committees and appoint committee chairs

  3. Executive compensation programs will be designed to ensure alignment of interest with the long-term interests of RHIO customers.

  4. Executive compensation will be fully disclosed.

  5. There will be a CEO succession plan.

  6. All directors will have access to senior management.

D. Roles of constituencies

  1. Advisory bodies will be established to ensure input from RHIO constituencies (e.g., RHIO customers, funding agencies, healthcare providers, regional interests, consumers).

  2. Role and reserve powers of RHIO

      a. As a source of credibility for RHIO, [founders] and their continuing support will be strongly visible.

      b. [Founders] will have specified reserve powers to ensure that the mission of the RHIO entity is carried out and that the RHIO entity is regularly accountable to [founders].

  3. Funding agencies

      a. The RHIO entity will maintain close, strong relationships with funding agencies.

  4. RHIO customers

      a. Contribute RHIO solutions to the RHIO entity

      b. Share RHIO costs on an equitable basis

    c. Leverage experience

    d. Participate in efforts to standardize and simplify RHIO functionality

5. Members of the public

    a. The RHIO entity will provide an opportunity for input from members of the public otherwise unaffiliated with RHIO customers and health benefits funding sources

Matrix of Entity and Governance Objectives and Principles Matched to Organization Options

Principle	Nonprofit Public Benefit Corporation		Nonprofit Mutual Benefit Corp.	Joint Powers Agency	Special Joint Powers Agency	For-Profit Entity
	501(c)(3)	501(c)(4)				
CHOICE OF ENTITY						
RHIO entity will be neutral to the interests of the various RHIO customers	Feasible	Feasible	Feasible	Feasible	Feasible	Not possible
The form of entity will permit membership to appoint directors	Possible	Possible	Possible	Feasible	Feasible	Possible
The form of entity will be tax exempt to the maximum extent possible	Possible	Possible	Possible	Possible	Possible	Not possible
The form of entity will be qualified to receive grants	Possible	Feasible	Not possible	Possible	Possible	Not possible
The form of entity will be perpetual	Possible	Possible	Possible	Possible	Possible	Possible
The form of entity will have a non-equity holding membership	Possible	Possible	Feasible[1]	Possible	Possible	Not possible
The RHIO entity will not be an extension or "creature" of governments	Possible	Possible	Possible	Not possible	Not possible	Possible

Principle	Nonprofit Public Benefit Corporation		Nonprofit Mutual Benefit Corp.	Joint Powers Agency	Special Joint Powers Agency	For-Profit Entity
	501(c)(3)	501(c)(4)				
CHOICE OF ENTITY (cont.)						
The RHIO entity may engage in limited political activity in an effort to influence legislation	Possible[2]	Possible	Possible	Not possible	Not possible	Possible
MEMBERSHIP						
Founders will identify who shall be authorized as members[3] and the RHIO entity's governing documents will grant that authority	Possible	Possible	Possible	Feasible	Feasible	Possible
All constituencies will be represented through membership	Possible	Possible	Possible	Feasible	Feasible	Feasible
Classes of membership may be established to establish different rights and duties for different members[4]	Possible	Possible	Possible	Feasible	Feasible	Possible
Members making a greater investment will have a major voice	Possible	Possible	Possible	Feasible	Feasible	Possible
The membership will elect the majority of the governing body[4]	Possible	Possible	Possible	Feasible	Feasible	Possible
Membership will grow and change to reflect growth and change in RHIO customers and in the uses of RHIO products	Possible	Possible	Feasible	Not possible	Feasible	Possible
GOVERNING BODY (BOARD OF DIRECTORS)						
The governing body will appoint and direct the RHIO entity officers	Possible	Possible	Possible	Possible	Possible	Possible

Principle	Nonprofit Public Benefit Corporation		Nonprofit Mutual Benefit Corp.	Joint Powers Agency	Special Joint Powers Agency	For-Profit Entity
	501(c)(3)	501(c)(4)				
GOVERNING BODY (BOARD OF DIRECTORS) (cont.)						
The governing body will establish and oversee implementation of policies regarding: RHIO product development; RHIO standardization; fees and charges; and vendor arrangements	Possible	Possible	Possible	Possible	Possible	Possible
The governing body will oversee financial performance	Possible	Possible	Possible	Possible	Possible	Possible
The governing body will appoint the independent auditors	Possible	Possible	Possible	Possible	Possible	Possible
The governing body will accommodate membership composition, growth and change	Possible	Possible	Feasible	Feasible	Feasible	Possible
Directors will be reflective in part of the RHIO customers	Possible	Possible	Possible	Feasible	Feasible	Possible
A significant number of directors will be independent; the governing body and the membership shall establish a common definition of "independence" (i.e., relationship to vendors, RHIO customers, funding sources)	Possible	Possible	Possible	Feasible	Feasible	Possible
Directors will represent diverse backgrounds and necessary skills	Feasible	Feasible	Feasible	Feasible	Feasible	Feasible
Management will be represented on the governing body	Possible	Possible	Possible	Feasible	Feasible	Possible
Founders will select some members of the governing body	Possible	Possible	Possible	Feasible	Feasible	Possible

Principle	Nonprofit Public Benefit Corporation		Nonprofit Mutual Benefit Corp.	Joint Powers Agency	Special Joint Powers Agency	For-Profit Entity
	501(c)(3)	501(c)(4)				
GOVERNING BODY (BOARD OF DIRECTORS) (cont.)						
Directors will be fiduciaries of the RHIO entity and not representatives of RHIO customers or other affiliations (i.e., neutral)	Feasible	Feasible	Feasible	Feasible	Feasible	Possible
The governing body will adopt written statements of its governance principles and code of conduct and regularly re-evaluate them	Possible	Possible	Possible	Possible	Possible	Possible
The governing body will establish written performance criteria and periodically review governing body performance against those criteria	Possible	Possible	Possible	Possible	Possible	Possible
The governing body will receive input from advisory boards of RHIO constituents (e.g., RHIO customers, funding agencies, healthcare providers, regional interests, enrollees)	Possible	Possible	Possible	Possible	Possible	Possible
Directors will have staggered terms, term limits and will serve without compensation	Possible	Possible	Possible	Feasible	Feasible	Possible
The governing body chair will be independent of management	Possible	Possible	Possible	Feasible	Feasible	Possible
The governing body will meet without management at least once per year	Possible	Possible	Possible	Possible	Possible	Possible

Principle	Nonprofit Public Benefit Corporation		Nonprofit Mutual Benefit Corp.	Joint Powers Agency	Special Joint Powers Agency	For-Profit Entity
	501(c)(3)	501(c)(4)				
GOVERNING BODY (BOARD OF DIRECTORS) (cont.)						
Audit, nomination, management evaluation, compliance and ethics functions will be carried out by non-management directors and committees supported by management	Possible	Possible	Possible	Feasible	Feasible	Possible
The Director nominating function will address: competing time commitments; continuing director tenure; openness to new ideas; willingness to critically re-examine the status quo; effective board size; qualification for re-nomination based on individual behavior expectations (e.g., attendance, preparedness, participation, candor and the input of the membership)	Possible	Possible	Possible	Feasible	Feasible	Possible
OFFICERS						
The CEO will • Provide management of day-to-day operations of the RHIO entity • Recommend policy and strategic direction of the RHIO entity for consideration by the governing body • Be spokesperson for the RHIO entity • Be a compensated executive	Possible	Possible	Possible	Feasible	Feasible	Possible

Principle	Nonprofit Public Benefit Corporation		Nonprofit Mutual Benefit Corp.	Joint Powers Agency	Special Joint Powers Agency	For-Profit Entity
	501(c)(3)	501(c)(4)				
OFFICERS (cont.)						
The governing body chair will • Conduct all meetings of the governing body and the membership • Oversee preparation of governing body and committee agendas • Define the quality, quantity, and timeliness of the flow of information between management and the governing body • Approve consultants who report directly to the governing body • Interview candidates for nomination as a director • Oversee development and revision of governance guidelines • Evaluate the CEO's performance • Recommend the composition of governing body committees and appoint committee chairs	Possible	Possible	Possible	Feasible	Feasible	Possible
Executive compensation programs will be designed to ensure alignment of interest with the long-term interests of RHIO customers	Possible	Possible	Possible	Possible	Possible	Possible

Principle	Nonprofit Public Benefit Corporation		Nonprofit Mutual Benefit Corp.	Joint Powers Agency	Special Joint Powers Agency	For-Profit Entity
	501(c)(3)	501(c)(4)				
OFFICERS (cont.)						
Executive compensation will be fully disclosed	Possible	Possible	Possible	Possible	Possible	Feasible
There will be a CEO succession plan	Possible	Possible	Possible	Possible	Possible	Possible
All directors will have access to senior management	Possible	Possible	Possible	Possible	Possible	Possible
ROLE OF CONSTITUENCIES						
Advisory bodies will be established to ensure input from RHIO software constituencies (e.g., RHIO customers, funding agencies, healthcare providers, regional interests, enrollees)	Possible	Possible	Possible	Feasible	Feasible	Possible
As a source of credibility for RHIO, XYZ and its continuing support will be strongly visible	Possible	Possible	Possible	Feasible	Feasible	Not possible
XYZ will have specified reserve powers to ensure that the mission of the RHIO entity with respect to the RHIO applications is carried out and that the RHIO entity is regularly accountable to XYZ	Possible	Possible	Possible	Feasible	Feasible	Not possible
The RHIO entity will maintain close, strong relationships with funding agencies	Possible	Possible	Possible	Possible	Possible	Possible

Principle	Nonprofit Public Benefit Corporation		Nonprofit Mutual Benefit Corp.	Joint Powers Agency	Special Joint Powers Agency	For-Profit Entity
	501(c)(3)	501(c)(4)				
ROLE OF CONSTITUENCIES (cont.)						
Certain funding agencies may condition grants on reserved oversight and approval rights	Possible	Possible	Not possible	Not possible	Not possible	Not possible
RHIO customers may contribute RHIO solutions to the RHIO entity; share RHIO software costs on an equitable basis; leverage experience; participate in efforts to standardize and simplify the RHIO software	Possible	Possible	Possible	Possible	Possible	Possible
The RHIO entity will provide an opportunity for input from members of the public otherwise unaffiliated with RHIO customers and health benefits funding sources	Possible	Possible	Possible	Possible	Possible	Possible

---

[1] However, the assets of a mutual benefit corporation are not irrevocably dedicated to public and/or charitable purposes and upon dissolution, or in connection with the repurchase or redemption of memberships, the corporation may distribute corporate assets to its members.

[2] However, providing support or opposition to a particular candidate for election is prohibited.

[3] "Membership" means the collective entities and individuals that are authorized to establish and maintain the governance structure of the RHIO entity and may have certain ultimate decision-making powers. Most members will also be RHIO customers. Founders may also be members.

[4] For example, counties could belong to Class A, granting standard rights and duties, and founders could belong to Class B, granting specific rights and/or duties, such as appointments to the governing body.

[5] "Governing body" means the group of individuals with ultimate authority for the management of the affairs of the RHIO entity.

Additional Resources: Health Information Exchange

Agency for Healthcare Research and Quality (AHRQ) National Resource Center for Health Information Technology:

http://healthit.ahrq.gov/portal/server.pt?open=512&objID=650&PageID=0&parentname=ObjMgr&parentid=106&mode=2&dummy=/index.html

AHRQ Evaluation Toolkit:

http://healthit.ahrq.gov/portal/server.pt/gateway/PTARGS_0_3882_81659_0_0_18/AHRQ%20NRC%20Evaluation%20Toolkit.pdf

- Agency for Healthcare Research and Quality
  Information from AHRQ-funded health IT projects, including a list of AHRQ-funded health information exchange (HIE) projects.
- AHRQ/Avalere Health LLC Report on Evolution of State Health Information Exchange: www.avalerehealth.net/research/

American Health Information Management Association (AHIMA): www.ahima.org

- eHIM® Resources: www.ahima.org/infocenter/ehim
- Health Information Exchange Resource Tool Kit: www.ahima.org/hie
- Other useful Web sites: www.ahima.org/hie/links.asp

American Medical Informatics Association:

www.amia.org/10x10/index.asp

Centers for Medicare & Medicaid Services (CMS)

Physician Focused Quality Initiative: www.cms.hhs.gov

Connecting for Health: http://connectingforhealth.org/resources/guidance.html
Markle Foundation: Model governmental and technical policy guidelines for HIE initiatives

Consumer League Response to National Health Information Exchange Network: www.nclnet.org/advocacy/health/hit_consumer_principles.pdf#search=%22health%20information%20exchange%22

eHealth Initiative (eHI): www.ehealthinitiative.org/
- **Connecting Communities for Better Health:**
  www.ehealthinitiative.org
  http://ccbh.ehealthinitiative.org/communities/funded.mspx
  eHealth Initiative
  Directory of HIE initiatives and a toolkit of model policies, agreements, forms, and other HIE resources
- **Connecting Communities Tool Kit:**
  http://toolkits.ehealthinitiative.org/
  eHealth Initiative
  Information for HIE start-ups; eHealth Initiative also tracks health IT and HIE legislation

Electronic Health Records Vendors Association (EHRVA): www.ehrva.org

Grants and Start-up Funding
- Office of National Health Information Technology Coordinator: http://www.hhs.gov/healthit
- Agency for Health Care Research and Quality: http://healthit.ahrq.gov/home/index.html
- Centers for Medicare & Medicaid Services (CMS), Physician Focused Quality Initiative: http://www.cms.hhs.gov
- eHealth Initiative Foundation, Connecting Communities for Better Health, Resource Center: http://ccbh.ehealthinitiative.org
- Connecting for Health, Markle Foundation: http://www.connectingforhealth.org
- Health eTechnologies Initiative, Robert Wood Johnson Foundation: http://www.hetinitiative.org
- American Medical Informatics Association: http://www.amia.org/10x10/index.asp

Healthcare Information & Management Systems Society (HIMSS): www.himss.org
- **HIT Dashboard:** www.hitdashboard.com/
  HIMSS and the Center for Health Information and Decision Systems
  Information about U.S. health IT programs, including RHIOs

Healthcare Information Technology Standards Panel—HITSP: www.hitsp.org

Integrating the Healthcare Enterprise (IHE): www.ihe.net

The Markle Foundation: www.markle.org/markle_programs/
The Markle Foundation's approach involves convening multi-sectoral groups of leaders and innovators from technology, government, public interest organizations and business to bring about the technical and policy changes needed to enable breakthroughs in the public interest. They typically seek out partners to help achieve their goals. Their current focus is on health and national security programs.

National Conference of State Legislatures: www.ncsl.org
- Forum for State Health Policy Leadership: www.ncsl.org/programs/health/forum
- Main health page: www.ncsl.org/programs/health/health.htm
- HIPAA page: www.ncsl.org/programs/health/HIPAA.htm
- State Health Notes: www.ncsl.org/programs/health/shn/subjindex.htm#hit

Patient Advocacy Groups:
- National Consumers League: www.nclnet.org/
- National Patient Safety Foundation: www.npsf.org

The Robert Wood Johnson Foundation: www.rwjf.org/index.jsp
The nation's largest philanthropy devoted to improving health and healthcare. RWJF supports training, education, research, and projects that demonstrate effective ways to deliver health services, especially for the most vulnerable among us.
What the RWJF funds: www.rwjf.org/applications/whatwefund.jsp

Sample Work Plan: www.dwt.com/practc/hit/publications.htm

Sources for Tracking Open RFP Solicitations:
- www.grants.gov
- www.fedbizopps.gov/
- www.ahrq.gov/fund/
- To obtain a D & B Registration (DUNS#): https://eupdate.dnb.com/requestOptions.html
- To obtain a Central Contractor Registration: http://www.ccr.gov

State RHIO Consensus Project: www/staterhio.org
AHIMA Foundation of Research and Education & NCSL Project funded through ONC grant. Provides report and guidebook to assist state-level HIE initiatives.

U.S. Department of Health and Human Services:
www.hhs.gov/healthinformationtechnology/
Portal to federal health IT efforts, including those under HHS (e.g., ONC, AHIC), the Department of Defense, and the Department of Veteran Affairs
- Office of the National Coordinator for Health Information Technology: www.hhs.gov/healthit/
- American Health Information Community: www.hhs.gov/healthit/ahic.html

Acronyms Used in This Guide

Acronym	Term
A³HIE	Ann Arbor Area Health Information Exchange
ADE	adverse drug event
ADT	admission discharge and transfer system
AHRQ	Agency for Healthcare Research and Quality
AMA	American Medical Association
ASCII	American Standard Code for Information Interchange
ASP	application service provider
ASTM	ASTM International (formerly American Society for Testing and Materials)
CCR	continuity of care record
CDR	clinical data repository
CMO	chief medical officer
CMS	Centers for Medicare & Medicaid Services
CHIN	community health information network
ED	emergency department
EHR	electronic health record
EMPI	enterprise master person index
EMR	electronic medical record
ePHI	electronic protected health information
EUHID	encrypted healthcare identifier
HEDIS	Health Plan Employer Data Information Set
HHS	Health and Human Services (U.S. Department of)
HIE	healthcare information exchange

Acronym	Term
HIPAA	Health Insurance Portability and Accountability Act
HIT	healthcare information technology
HL7	Health Level 7
ID	identifier
IDN	integrated delivery network
IHIE	Indiana Health Information Exchange
IRC	Internal Revenue Code
IRS	Internal Revenue Service
IT	information technology
LIS	laboratory information system
LLC	limited liability company
LHII	local health information infrastructure
LOUHIE	Louisville Health Information Exchange, Inc.
MA-SHARE	Massachusetts Simplifying Healthcare Among Regional Entities
MDS	minimal data sets
MHIN	Michiana Health Information Network
MINE	Medical Information Network Exchange
MOU	memorandum of understanding
MPI	master person index
NEHEN	New England Healthcare EDI Network
NHII	national health information infrastructure
NHIN	national health information network
NORC	National Opinion Research Center
NPP	notice of privacy practices
OHCA	organized health care arrangement
OIG	Office of Inspector General (U.S.)
ONC	Office of the National Coordinator of Health Information Technology
ORS	operating room system
PFSH	personal, family, and social histories
PHI	protected health information
PHR	personal health record
RBAC	role-based access control
RFP	request for proposal
RHIN	regional health information network
RHIO	regional health information organization
RIS	radiology information systems
RLS	record locator service
ROI	return on investment
RWJF	Robert Wood Johnson Foundation
SDK	software development kit
SLA	service level agreements
SQL	Structured Query Language

Acronym	Term
SSN	Social Security number
SWOT	strengths, weaknesses, opportunities, threats
UHID	universal healthcare identifier
UHIN	Utah Health Information Network
UMS	Unified Medical Schema
UPO	user principal object
VIA	virtual identifier aggregation
VNHID	voluntary national healthcare identifier
VPN	virtual private network
VPO	virtual patient object
WAN	wide area network
XML	extensible markup language

Index